MW00873468

"LOVE UNDER THE KOLA NUT TREE.
WHAT CITY MOMS DIDN'T TELL YOU ABOUT CREATING
FULFILLING RELATIONSHIPS"
ONLINE MEMBERSHIP SITE CERTIFICATE:

Esther Lamnyam and The Entrée and Dance Club
(http://entreeanddanceclub.com)
invites you to continue the
conversation. To register and for more information, go
to http://estherlamnyam.com
Use Reference # **922P2184** when you register.
(It gives you free access for a limited period of time)
Membership Site By Imitate Nature, LLC

Imitate Nature . Become Daily

Strive To Be Happy.

Powerful Tools On How To

(Your blueprint to generating the energy and charge you need to be continuously creative and productive.)

Esther Lamnyam

Publishing By Imitate Nature, LLC

Disclaimer and Legal Notices:
The information presented herein presents the view of the author at the date of publication. The author reserves the right to alter and update her opinion based on new conditions as they arise. This publication is for informational purposes only. If advice concerning legal, health, or related matters is needed, the services of a fully qualified professional should be sought. This publication is not intended for use as a source of legal business practices in your country or state. Any reference to any person or business, whether living or dead, is purely coincidental.

ISBN-13: 978-1494286576
ISBN-10: 1494286572

The author's website: www.estherlamnyam.com

Esther Lamnyam is a consultant, speaker, author, healer, Wellness & Life Success Strategist, Iridologist, and IT Systems Architect. Contact her for volume copies, speaking engagements, workshops, and other engagements by going to her website or by sending an email to info@ImitateNature.com.
Esther is the founder of Imitate Nature Consulting and Coaching International, and The Entrée and Dance Club:
http://entreeanddanceclub.com
email: info@ImitateNature.com

Sites of interest:
http:/loveunderthekolanuttree.com
http://www.youtube.com/user/elylams
Peter Vermeeren's website: http://www.bumon.es
Cover Design by Elle Designs:
http://elledesignsblog.wordpress.com
Edited by Tressa Janik
www.Tressa.me
Author's picture by Mary Fletcher

ALSO BY ESTHER LAMNYAM

Love Under the Kola Nut Tree. What City Moms Didn't Tell You About Creating Fulfilling Relationships.

My Husband Is A Cuckoo. And Other Poems of my Youth

A Fable: How The Dog Became A Domestic Animal And Two Bonus Fables (Kindle eBook)

Cracking the Code, The Path to Creating a Successful Life, Powerful Tools to Bring about Life Fulfillment, and A Home Study Coaching Program

Dedication

Dedicated to YOU... the reader!

We are all connected; without your reading this, the blog post(s) (http://estherlamnyam.com/strive-to-be-happy-%E2%80%93-twelve-powerful-secrets-on-how-to) (http://tinyurl.com/kvjajhg) **and your feedback, only the wind would hear me. Would I be encouraged to speak or write if the wind was my only audience?**

Gratitude

Thanks to all my teachers, Sophia, and experiences!

Heartfelt thanks to Peter Vermeeren, who has been working with me virtually and insisted I create this product. All my teachers have said so, but you brought more light enabling me to do it and waited patiently for me to create it! You are the feather that finally tipped the scale. Thank you for your light; May the LORD, God, replenish it daily as you give to others.

Contents

15

Introduction

A personal message from Wellness and Life Success Strategist Esther Lamnyam:

Hello! This is Esther Lamnyam, author of the book *"Love Under the Kola Nut Tree. What City Moms Didn't Tell You About Creating Fulfilling Relationships."* A blog I wrote entitled <u>Strive to Be Happy – Twelve Powerful Secrets on How to</u> generated lots of interest and also requests to write for other blogs. Here is the link to it, though I will paste the contents below for those who cannot link online while reading this or are reading this in hard copy: <u>http://estherlamnyam.com/strive-to-be-happy-%E2%80%93-twelve-powerful-secrets-on-how-to/</u> (<u>http://tinyurl.com/kvjajhg</u>).

Due to the amount of interest, I have decided to give you more tips on how to juice up your life in a little book format. In *"Love Under the Kola Nut Tree. What City Moms Didn't Tell You About Creating Fulfilling Relationships"*, the queen Maya Sophia encouraged Mariyah and her friends to be happy by examining themselves; the light and juice is within. In response to some of the characters in the book's complaints about others for example she would say:

"You mean to tell me you were single for more than thirty years, then God blessed you with a good man and you punish him for not taking out the trash? What happened to your hands?" - Quote from Love Under the Kola Nut Tree.

17

So as a pre-requisite or post-requisite for this little book, buy *and read* the book *"Love Under the Kola Nut Tree. What City Moms Didn't Tell You Creating Fulfilling Relationships,"* by moi ☺ Esther Lamnyam! This quote from "Love Under the Kola Nut Tree," applies to the concepts discussed in this text:

She would say, "some of these things I tell you might not make sense, but I am leaving soon and I have to tell you these things so you can improve your life and that of the lives of the generation to come. Listen, even if it does not make sense now. Be like the goat, which eats lots of grass in the daytime or in good weather then at night regurgitates and chews on it well. Meditate on these things I tell you with an open mind later and ask for light to be poured on it for illumination."

I tried to keep these tips succinct; use them as a point of departure to the larger world the concept brings to light.

Cheers to happiness!

Esther

18

Starting with Definitions

What does it mean to be happy? Let's see the dictionary definition below:

http://www.merriam-webster.com/dictionary/happy
Happy - adjective \ˈha-pē

: Feeling pleasure and enjoyment because of your life, situation, etc.
: Showing or causing feelings of pleasure and enjoyment
: Pleased or glad about a particular situation, event, etc.

====================///====================

http://www.merriam-webster.com/dictionary/joy

Definition of JOY

1(a).) The emotion evoked by well-being, success, or good fortune or by the prospect of possessing what one desires: delight

(b).) The expression or exhibition of such emotion: gaiety

2.) A state of happiness or felicity: bliss

3.) A source or cause of delight

Related to JOY

Synonyms

Beatitude, blessedness, bliss, blissfulness, felicity, gladness, happiness, warm fuzzies

Antonyms

Calamity, ill-being, misery, sadness, unhappiness, wretchedness

Happiness: It also describes happiness as: a state of well-being and contentment: **joy**

"Village" Approach:

Villagers just use the tools nature has provided them. So we do this here in this text as well. To get to happiness, joy is the undercurrent.

We all have different definitions for happiness based on our experiences and culture for what makes us feel truly yummy inside.

Get joy and happiness, let bliss and other good stuff flow in! Thus happiness seems to be a pre-requisite for lots of beautiful things.

Joy is very important for many reasons. Very simply, it is necessary for good mental, physical, and spiritual alertness, which enables us to be vastly productive. As an iridologist and coach, I see many people whose business, relationships, health, and more has been marred because they did not have the energy provoked and invoked by joy.

I remember very distinctly a gentleman from Baltimore who consulted with me. He told me how he had lost so much zeal; and because of his relationships issues, he kept procrastinating to follow up on a letter he had received from the local government about one of his real estate properties. By the time he mustered the energy and desire to check on it, the property had been foreclosed on him! He was very sad about this.

So this is a serious topic!

Other real examples:

- Joyless people have not given a good performance on stage, thus losing great opportunities

- Joyless workers who are brilliant but perform abysmally and end up losing contracts. Most of the time due to failing relationships.
- Joyless gentleman who would not exercise to get better because he was getting back at his wife and family; he ended up in a wheel chair.
- Joyless teen that refused to wake up early for a sports meet thus was not given a scholarship and ended up struggling most of their life (All they needed to do was show up at the field at 7 a.m. to qualify and the scholarship was theirs because that is how good they were).

In *"Love Under the Kola Nut Tree. What City Moms Didn't Tell You about Creating Fulfilling Relationships,"* we learn that there are laws of nature or of the universe, as some would say, and there are man-made laws. You have to integrate the two to be successful on this earthly plane. For example, if you pray for a scholarship and the spiritual or universal principles connive or work together to get you a sports meet. YOU have to follow the man-made laws and show up at this drill so law suits (man-made principles) do not complicate issues.

I could give you more real experience examples, but these will suffice for now and as we go through the ways to strive to be happy, more examples as related will be discussed.

Joy gives us strength. Even in a battle, you need the undercurrent of joy to be truly "angry" to fight. Joy helps us deal with silly people and traffic.

There are lots of books and tools on the same topic – being happy (diamond ring anyone?) Use them. Use what works for you. Here I give you practical application tools. They are

22

nature tested and nature certified. There are not exotic but "battlefield" tools to move the dial for you! Because, they work! Try them. Do it! Please give us feedback at: www.imitatenature.com so others can use and benefit from your experience. We are all in this together. Your happiness in the interconnectedness of this world will eventually flow to me and mine to you. (Remember how the atrocities perpetrated against school children affects us all... the one not-so-happy person destroyed the innocence of many!)

Do not underestimate how simple these tools are. Nature's power is in its simplicity. If you truly desire to get that current of energy flowing within you and pull on it to create your desires, here are the tools for you, which you sought.

Definitely, please consult your trained and licensed physician or counselor for your clinical health. Tools in this book should not be substituted for a licensed physician or counselor. Herein is a villager's approach to living a happy life. If grandma or grandpa told the villager to drink a bowl of water first thing in the morning after swirling it with their index finger to heal an ailment, the village will thank granny profusely and go do it and be healed. We really, through our belief, do our own healing. However, in the world we live in today, we need disclaimers for much!

In addition, this book will be your little pocket guide for bliss. **You** and only **you**, are responsible for your happiness! Do not put that on another human being born of woman. All born of woman have issues to deal with, even the best of us. Teach this to your kids, family, students, congregations, and countrymen.

In this book, I bring simple tools born out of nature and from working with people and learning from their issues, discontent, and mindsets. Learning from the valleys, hills, molehills, mountains, and voids of my journey also has fine-tuned these tools. Consider the murderously angry partner, angry because her husband went to play golf or to study. She wants him to stay home, sit on the couch with his arms around her, watch TV, and giggle together. Or consider the man with same desires from his partner . How can you maintain your happiness if you have one of these partners?

Let's find out...

Strive to Be Happy – More Powerful Secrets on How to

Here is the blog post that is the genesis for this book, let's start there:

From: http://estherlamnyam.com/strive-to-be-happy-%E2%80%93-twelve-powerful-secrets-on-how-to (http://tinyurl.com/kvjajhg)

Strive to Be Happy – Twelve Powerful Secrets on How to.
I received an early morning call from someone in a not so happy place today. There are a few tools to get one out of a not so happy place. I'll give you twelve here:

1. Sing a song or just sing "doe– a deer, a female deer; ray– a drop of golden sun; me– a name I call myself; far– a long, long way to run; … etc." from The Sound of Music. By the time you sing it the third time your energy and that around you would have changed. Try it! Vowel sounds are the secret to the universe and to changing the atmosphere. (Vowel sounds are so powerful, creative, and have such high vibrational energy some languages do not use them!) Tune yourself!!!

2. Listen to Music. Music can heal and bring joy and more. Soon you will be dancing or tapping your toes in rhythm with the music.

3. Call your name. The power in your name is so enormous! Most of us never call our name or even own it! I can get things done in the name of someone (mom, dad, boss, Jesus, supervisor, etc.). Try getting things done in your name! (More on this later in another blog) But attune with it (your name) first. (Names are so powerful that some steal it! Has yours been stolen?)

4. Do something for someone else; take the focus off of you and

25

your problem.

5. Alter your mind and alter your life. Where your thoughts and mind go…your countenance will follow. Fantasize. Imagine.

6. Talk a walk…nature has a way of cleansing, purifying, and opening our awareness. Use the natural elements…they are free!

7. Hang out with kids! They are powerful change agents with good energy that just take over the room!!

8. Long term: Set goals and work daily towards accomplishing them. When you have a purpose you dwell on it instead of on your problem.

9. Fake it! Yes, you heard me right. Your subconscious mind does not know when you are faking… Ah ha! Soon it starts doing the real thing…so laugh it out! Pretend to be happy! (Read more in "Love Under the Kola Nut Tree.")

10. Get in touch with your God and the Master within. He promised to comfort and to bring joy, and all those promises have been kept and are still being kept daily!

11. Remember, this too shall pass…it always does.

12. Well, if you need a little 'magic,' use the laws of nature…. just spin them eggs as in "Love Under the Kola Nut Tree. What City Moms Didn't Tell You About Creating Fulfilling Relationships." Link to video on how to spin eggs: http://www.youtube.com/watch?v=EgntLUkWR14

Strive to be happy. Joy is needed to create!

Posted December 13, 2010

Now Let's Update This Blog List with More Powerful Secrets on How to Be Happy:

*Choice. Choose; decide to be happy. Our conscious choices gives permission to the elements of nature, our subconscious mind, ethereal beings to work in tandem with us, delivering joy yet untold! Decide. Choose this day to be...

Never satisfied? Learn to be content in whatever situation. Every situation in our lives presents a learning opportunity. It is a tool and a gift to get us to the next level on our life journey. However, if we do not look at it that way, we will cause havoc in our lives and in the lives of others. We will only keep going round and round the block until we learn the lesson, so we move to the next level --- with its own challenges!

Accept people for who they are. Trying to change people is hardly successful. Save yourself a headache and work on **you**!

Fable example. Muring - The Girl Who Married the Head:
Villagers teach kids lifelong lessons via fables, folktales, proverbs, and parables. Here is one about how not accepting people for who they are lead a spoilt-diva-bitchy princess to become the laughing stock for centuries.

27

Muring - The Girl Who Married the Head

The chief of a village had a very beautiful daughter. She was very, very beautiful and all the beautiful trinkets, oils, ornaments, and makeup brought by rich kings, princes, and suitors from far and wide only made her more beautiful. Her maids massaged herbs and oils on her, braided her long locks, and put jewelry all over her. As she came of age, suitors lined up to propose to her.

However, she was full of her beautiful self and was never satisfied with the men who proposed to her. Their legs were either too big, or their nose, or ears or mouth were too big, or their butt or hands and fingers too large. If two men stood in front of her one with smaller hands, guess what she would say to both of them, "your hands are too big!" Very simply, in the village they now say, if a woman does not like you, she would say everything about you is…"too big!" (Villagers do not have a word for "love".)

As the years went by, this princess refusing all suitors provoked a "traffic jam" of some sort in marriage land. In that village, the elder children married before the younger in the palace. So her not accepting a marriage proposal from any suitors meant her younger siblings could not marry. Thus she was not well liked even in the palace. Even the king was frustrated, as he could not form alliances through her marriage or of his other kids because she was 'blocking' by being too picky!

She had to be married so her dowry of cowries could be used to marry wives for the sons.

News of her beauty and ego spread through the clan and beyond like wild fire. Challenge a young man with raging hormones on how to win a woman and the game is on! So men came from far and wide with their best game to no avail. There were those who could climb a tree upside down. Those who could herd a flock of birds! Those who could sing in a hundred voices like a choir, at the same time. You name it. However, none impressed her.

28

In a faraway village, a warrior who only survived death during a battle due to his prowess and magical powers heard of this girl. Being a man of battle, he loved challenges. Unfortunately for him, the last battle left him all amputated; that is, all except his head. Let's call him The Head. He grew locks and trained his mind, teeth, tongue, and locks to do amazing feats.

He also became interested in this damsel. When some of his villagers heard this, some laughed and some forecasted the princess Muring had finally asked for it.

The Head listened to all of what had transpired and being a strategist, he knew Muring very well now. How would The Head travel to another village? How would he win the hand of a princess to whom all men fell short and who was never satisfied? Well, he developed **a plan**.

He rolled his head to the strongest builders' house and borrowed the man's arms and hands promising to return them within a few days. The strong builder gave his arms and hands to The Head.

He rolled his head to the tallest man's house and begged to borrow his limbs for a few days. The man obliged.

He thought of people with the best body parts that could entice a never satisfied woman. He borrowed all the appendages and a torso and walked confidently into the palace decked in garb borrowed from the finest weavers. Even the spiders would have been jealous! He did not even have much to offer compared to other suitors, all he had was the traditional nine calabashes of palm wine, 40 liters of palm oil, kola nuts, and whiskey for the ancestors.

He did not even woo and pledge to her and make promises. He simply stated why he was there like all the other men, simply to win the hand of the most beautiful woman in the world, a princess that made the moon strive to be even more beautiful!

Palace gatherers who came daily for free food and drinks from all the suitors thought this brother had lost his mind.

Traditionally his gifts were what ordinary folks came to ask for a daughter's hand in marriage with. But Muring had raised the level of proposal gifts to unheard of items. Parents with boy children hated her for this precedent she had set.

The Head smiled at Muring; bowed before the king and asked for his precious daughter's hand in marriage. The king responded as usual,

"My son, we are honored to drink the palm wine of your proposal. However, my wives and I are only babysitters of children who belong to God and to the village." He paused, drank more wine and had his cup, made of cow tusk horn, filled three more times with the delicious palm wine that The Head had brought.

"You have to ask Muring herself. If a young woman does not say, "yes" to a suitor's marriage proposal, our customs prohibit us from accepting a dowry on her".

By now the routine was familiar. This particular palm wine was very good, just the right amount of alcohol, strong enough for men, yet sweet enough for women. People drank quickly before the next suitor's wine replaced it. They knew Muring would, as usual, say,

"Hummm marry who? Me? Shuut." Then she would smack her teeth in disgust and say,

"Look at your big feet, or big eyebrows, or big forehead. Please. Do I look like some princess who wants kids with big heads, big shoulders, big toes…?" and smack her teeth again.

In some cases when the suitor was full of airs, Muring would get up and parade the room, shaking the trinkets on her waist and arms. Dancing exotic traditional moves to show off to this full-of-himself suitor what he was not capable of having and what he would be missing. She wanted her image imprinted in his mind to mess up his future relationships.

Men were known to go crazy from desire after meeting her face to face. She would at times giggle with her maids or have them

30

dance for her or with her. Many men in palace court attendance only came to enjoy Muring's theatrics. Many of the elders secretly enjoyed her turning suitors away. Many men, especially those who were of families that could not marry her and the older men, secretly did not want her to marry as her beauty, body, dance moves, and sensuality were the only mental stimulus they now lived for. Their wives were old, taking care of babies, or working on the farm too much and these men welcomed Muring's theatrics.

For the same behavior, some hated her while some loved her for it. To each his own.

But things were about to change. The Head and all in court waited for Muring to start her tirade of reasons why she would not marry The Head. These had become so poetic, they were being rehearsed on every farm, school yard, boy and girl exchange… "Eh, eh, he, he, he, eeehhh, (smack teeth), look at your big nose," then walk away swinging her butt, shaking her boobs.

Muring did not respond. The silence went on too long, and her father, the king thought for once she might have dosed off in court. He looked at the handsome Head and motioned him with the raise of his eyebrows to ask his daughter's hand directly from her. The Head said to her,

"Princess Muring, when I look into your eyes I wonder how many oceans are in them. I want to sail in the oceans of your eyes…with you. I hear you sing melodious songs, I long to hear you sing all day in our compound to our beautiful children that only an amazing beauty like you can bear. Even the seasons will obey you. I may not have all the wealth of the other suitors, but I present my head to you …all I have is my head. All that I have in it is yours." Hehehe! Men! (Hint: believe what people tell you.)

Muring blushed, squirmed in her throne, and adjusted the trinkets and cowries over her chest and head.

Eh? What is happening? Her father and the chief's wives

31

allowed in court that day held the wine they had just sipped in their mouths, too alert to swallow. "Is Muring okay?" They were so used to Muring saying no, they did not even remember there was an alternative to the answer "no".

Everyone else who was an opportunist kept drinking. "This suitor's wine is very delicious, let me drink real quick before Muring slaps him with her curses and they replace it with the next suitor's wine," they said to themselves.

Well, Muring accepted his proposal no questions asked! No poetic curses, insulting moves, provocative dance, or laughter. No "big" this or that body part! Just a young girl blushing; even bashful to stare into the suitor's eyes as she had done with the other suitors.

Normally, in this culture, the suitor returned a few times with his parents and elders to negotiate the bride pride and bring livestock, palm oil, salt, and blankets. But today was a new day! The king, fearing his daughter might change her mind after finally accepting a marriage proposal, had prepared all the necessary rituals. (Get this kid out of here! ☺ Watch nature channels… eat for free for a while; learn to hunt for yourself, and then it is time to leave! Get out!)

The Head was asked to indulge the chief and stay for the week of festivities and only send for his folks.

The village and neighboring villages went into frenzy. People wanted to know whom this man was who finally won Muring's heart. Since he came from a faraway village, they attributed his not being recognized to that. Little did they know real drama was about to unfold!

Instead of the suitor giving gifts to people, people were giving gifts to him! Muring's brothers were already in love with him. This was a man, a real man! Many young men planned to come under his tutelage to learn how to charm a diva, a 'bitch', and woman! Her brothers sent messages to the girls they had wanted to marry and

32

Strive To Be Happy. Powerful Tools On How To

now would soon marry to know that one of their future kids had to be named after this suitor - The Head. They started preparing their marriages in earnest.

The marriage ceremony was done, the verbal contracts were made, and dances took place day and night. Cows, goats, and chickens were killed and delicacies served. Other chiefs and sub chiefs came with their gifts and entourages. The palace was crowded; young men found brides among the ladies who showed up displaying their beauty. The young people and parents could now breathe a sigh of relief!

After the festivities, Muring and her bevy of maids left the palace with loads of wealth to start her new life. She was in love and glowed even more beautifully. Maidens danced her off all the way to the boundary of the village.

It took them two days of trekking to get to The Head's village. On the outskirt, they met a man with no arms rushing towards The Head.

"Man, what took you so long? I missed a project because you have my arms. I need to work so I can have money for my kids' hunting gear. He plucked his arms off The Head and hurried away.

Muring and her maids were in shock. She screamed and asked her maids to turn around and return home.

"You are my wife now, the dowry has been paid." The Head said and nudged her with his legs towards his village. Muring started sobbing. Surely this was a trick; a man cannot be without arms she comforted herself.

Next another man showed up without legs, before Muring could scream, her husband removed his longs legs and gave it to the man, thanking him profusely with gifts and kola nuts for loaning him his legs. He was sure the majestic height the legs afforded him had helped him in winning Muring's hand in marriage.

33

© 2014 Esther Lamnyam

Muring started hyperventilating. She turned to her maids for support and a plan of escape, but found out only a few were still with her. Some hated her being such a spoiled woman who was only concerned about her own happiness. Now they could escape her tyranny and finally get married.

"Take me back home," she screamed arrogantly.

"Remember, you cannot go back there. Your dowry has been paid. You are no longer a person allowed to live there. Even your father told you not to come back there, as it is not your home anymore", one of her maids said to her.

Being from the palace, she was aware of that custom. Once married, you were no longer a part of the village. Girls who had ran back home from abusive partners had been told to return to their husbands, as there was no room for them in their parent's home, and no farm for them to farm. The farms were given or reserved for the wives of the sons. Muring had perpetuated this custom, because that was all she knew. Now she was a victim of it herself. Her bad behavior flashed before her eyes. Years of being an arrogant diva, just because she was born in the palace limited her vision and compassion. Now, by some natural law, she was being punished!

She could not even do dishes, nor cook, nor wash her clothes, or her underwear nor work on a farm.

As she was coming to her senses, news had spread earlier in the week that The Head had married the "full-of-it" beautiful princess. The villagers came out with puzzled looks on their faces and lined the streets...they wanted to see who could marry a head.

The Head, meanwhile, was finally striped to a head. By then Muring had no maid left with her. They were all scared of a man becoming a head in front of their own eyes. They threw away her trinkets that she could not even carry and disappeared quietly into the farms. Some ran away with her luxury items.

They came to a lonely tiny, tiny hut, and The Head motioned

34

for her to get in, "this is your new home".

When she refused and tried to run away, this fighter of a head, head butted her into the hut... her new home!

That is how the folktale ends!

(Well, a song was made out of this story, as villagers do.)

P.S. They now say in the village, "if a woman does not like a man, everything about him is big!" Sometimes when I listen to discussions on TV, especially in the leadership arenas, when someone is being harshly criticized no matter what...I will say, "everything about him is big."

"Seems everything about me today is big," a partner in the doghouse says. Because when the tides turn, the person   becomes likable ('small') again. So the day your partner is pissed, just say, "hmmm...darling, looks like everything about me is big, oh!" Get it? Hehehe.

(You will read the story about the jealous wife and husband below to make this point even more humorous)

Lesson: We force people to become whom they are not in order to receive our love. Once they snap back into place...all nature does...we do not like them anymore! By then, we might have burned our bridges or the years have taken their toll and we are not so cute anymore.... Thus,

Accept people for who they are. This will limit your frustrations and increase your being happy quotient.

Rituals. Have a ritual you practice daily. This will help

position you and give you your bearings for your present location. It could be something as simple as when you get to work every morning go wash your hands before starting work. Or when you come home you take five to fifteen minutes of "me grounding"

35

time. This settles you, changes your consciousness, and snaps you to your present locale and task. Your family and work will love you for it, as they will benefit the rewards of a more centered you.

The pleasure of giving pleasure. When we give, especially from the heart, happiness flows in. We feel good. Give a hug, a smile, a helping hand, a t-shirt to another child, shoes, money, or baby-sit. Most giving is not very comfortable, as it takes us out of our comfort zone but the benefits to all outweighs the discomfort.

Improve your self-esteem. Self –esteem is mostly about how we look at ourselves. How we mentally perceive "self". No one can disrespect (diss) you and be effective if you do not receive it. Honor you, love you, and work on parts of you that you deem need working on. Get a coach if you need to. People would write and say things about you, and then they move on to the next target and story. Only you turn their words into reality by how you absorb and react to them. People who write evil understand "belief and faith". They have faith that YOU will take their words and cook them until they poison your insides. You do the real work!

Strive to understand others. Misconception brings a lot of heartache and unhappiness. Even if you think someone is "crazy" at least now you know who he or she is, and you will know how to better handle him or her. If you understand someone's "craziness" and still complain, then the "crazy" one might be looking at you and say you are "crazy."

Do not take others and partners for granted. Just because someone promised to love you forever does not mean you can slack off. Even God changes His mind. They have the choice to leave the relationship any given day; do not encourage them to harbor such thoughts if you want to be with them. Say please and thank you. Apologize. If they cook for you and wash your laundry, boy blow them kisses and tell them how much you appreciate those gestures. Many broken hearts are born from being ungrateful. Even God says, "Praise Me, call my name, do not murmur, or grumble"! Hehehe! If He needs it, what more can be expected from an earthling with memories of all childhood issues and baggage to fill the trunk of your car?

Relationships are a choice. Know all involved have the ability to un-choose you. Nobody is stuck with another. When we abuse and choose to not honor relationships and other humans, they might leave us if they have enough self-confidence. We, thus, architect our own unhappiness.

Speak out loud, prophesize unto thyself good things.
Call goodness into your life; command things that do not work in your life to leave you. This is very powerful, but most of us do not do it or forget. I have come to believe there are invisible "creatures" programmed to show up if we set the right atmosphere. Once they show up, they will do what has been programmed in them to do. But you have to set the atmosphere for them to show up. Example: If I want a fruit fly to show up, I let a banana get overripe! If I want water to show up, I cover hot food with a lid and that lid gets laden with water! Use nature's programming code to your success.

Dance. Dancing moves energy, pumps blood and oxygen into our system, refreshes us, and more. The vibrations provoked, raise our energy to "happiness and above" levels. Best of all, join my Entrée and Dance club where we connect with sound, instruments, and food to make things come into fruition in our lives at http://entreeanddanceclub.com. Movement is the modus operandi of creation and nature. Everything keeps moving; stagnation gives 'death' a welcome.

Smile, laugh, and pretend to be happy.
Excerpt from Love Under the Kola Nut Tree:

"Belief is exactly what you call it; start with blind faith. Pretend until you believe it. The more you raise your aspirations, the more you will be able to pull the invisible into the visible. For example, when you build a house it is first a formless thought, and then visualization; lastly, you pull it into visible dense matter with bricks, stones, and wood."

As an eight-year-old, I loved to play and had lots of playmates. One particular eight-year-old boy named Kialep nagged, cried, whined, and complained all the time. One day after school I went to his compound to play; as I followed him around, he followed his father whining and crying seeking goodies and affection.

"I just want to play; come on, Kialep, let's play."

His father, a pastor, stopped and turned around, gave him a stern glare and said, "Kialep, pretend to be happy." Even at that age, I knew that was a profound command."

Be with Trees. Trees are present, beautiful, powerful, graceful, and cleansing. Talk a walk in nature.

Listen to different kinds of music than you would listen to. Soothing music's vibrations, resonance, overtones, and daydreaming from the lyrics will take your mind off what is bothering you. Music in a foreign language enables you to dwell

on the melody and vibrations, and not words that might affect your emotions more.

Take a shower after leaving crowded places, meetings, and churches (even Jesus was hit with energy!). Then rub yourself with some olive oil, sweet smelling oil, perfume, or flowers. Sometimes we pick up energy that keeps us unhappy; thus pay attention and you will begin to know who and where to stay away from or pray before, during, and after an encounter.

Grieve, sing a dirge, mourn, cry, weep, sob, recite, or make up poetry as you cry. Talk. Tell a story; recount the relationship whether good or bad that passed, scream, lament, bless, or pour your heart out. Then let it go! Bathe thereafter and anoint self with olive oil or blessed oil. We live in a society when people have made crying a weakness, so it either has to be sexy or a way to show remorse to get leniency. Many have ignored the healing and releasing power of crying. Like my girlfriend, Nene, who said, "thank 'goodness' for menopause", as now she can cry effortlessly. Welcome to the club my dear!

    With negative energy released, she has much clarity and she is at peace with herself and others. Do not wait for menopause, have a good cry if you are hurting; do it in the car if you think you will embarrass your house mates or that they will be embarrassed by you crying. You might be surprised if they join you and you all get free therapy... hehehe. Thus give yourself permission to grieve small and big losses; wail, it clears the path for forward movement.

Create a healing circle with two or more people. Stick to whatever needs to be resolved, leave the past alone!

Let it go! Drop things on the ground. The earth keeps spinning. Do not hold on to bygones. No one will ever be able to repay you. **Seek** better Kingdoms.

Use your real name or your power name. (Repeat point) When you vibrate and intone your name, more forces stand at attention at your disposal. If using your short or endearing name (such as Bill, AJ), make sure you like that name.

In an African fable, the turtle is loaned wings by the birds for a visit to a king who lives in the sky. The turtle advises them to all get names to introduce themselves to the sky king. He conveniently calls himself "All Of You." During their visit, when offered food and gifts, he always asked the host, "Who is this for?" and the host replied, "It is for 'all of you'." So he hoarded all to himself.

On their return trip, the very hungry and angry birds took their feathers away from him and he crashed to the earth shattering his shell to the many pieces, which you see glued together today!

Name! Think about a name. Call it. How does it make you feel? Imagine that individual with a different name.

Excerpt from "_My Husband Is a Cuckoo and Other Poems of My Youth_" By Esther Lamnyam

What's in a Name?

Give a baby a name,
it grows with it.
Give a thing a name,
it is known by it.
What's in a name?

There is trust in a name
when the bearer is just and courageous.
There is confidence in a name
when the bearer is kind in thoughts.
There is love in a name
when the bearer gives kindly.
There is gentleness in a name
when the bearer sacrifices and
does not take for granted.

What's in a name?
I'll tell you.

Fear is in a name
when it belongs to a tyrant;

everyone shivers when it is pronounced.
There is excitement in a name
when that name brings warmth and comfort.
There is reputation in a name
when the bearer is one of great deeds
when the bearer has great achievements.

What's in a name?
A name has personality
when the bearer is subtle,
when he is highly individual in behavior.
There is credit in a name,
it has honor and influence.
Yes, it has power, based on the trust of others.

What's in a name?
There is shame in a name
when the name provokes consciousness of guilt,
when it brings disgrace.

A name!
Keep it, tend it, build it,
you'll live by it.

A name!
Soil it, destroy it,
you'll die by it.

What's in a name?
Wait, I'll tell you,
plenty.

To testimonial or not to testimonial? Know the medium to make testimonials. 1. Sometimes information is shared too early when getting into relationships. Imitate the sun... do not shade the noon's strength of rays in the early morning. 2. Unhappiness sometimes springs from not being able to succeed in studies we have paid classes for. A second look though, shows we attended all the classes, but, more time was spent in testimonial discussion as opposed to content mastering. One hour of lecture content becomes reduced to five minutes of hurried summary at the end because of testimonials.

Many begin to self-doubt their ability to learn and other's self-confidence wanes. The trainer/teacher/coach/counselor, etc., loses clients though they have top-notch material. Next time they offer a class/webinar/seminar/weight training, etc., clients dodge.

You have to be using a 'slanted' observation to see this point, and that it is the cause of much unhappiness especially when others are affected. If someone came to you to figure out this issue of say a failing business or poor grades, you probably have to shadow them to discern this issue. As an example: not grasping metric system conversion and erroneously half filling a plane with fuel because of wrong conversion due to the fact that not enough time was focused on comprehending metrics. Unhappiness also stems from constantly stressing over one's job

43

because of not having the proper knowledge and understanding. The genesis of the resulting unhappiness is sometimes difficult to determine!

Another point about testimonials: though very much needed in advertisement and in creating credibility for a product, however, in ordinary discussions, turning discussion points into personal testimonials or as applied to you, limits constructive debates. This is because others fear objective observations are now being taken as directed criticism. This makes people unhappy because they end up not getting their point or genius idea across. Be like the goat, just chew on this point and when you experience it, you will digest it even more. Mind the medium.

Stop saying, "I know" (to stop the explanation) when being given instruction, as it eliminates learning the basics. Hang in tight and swallow the explanatory steps ...again. Within the basic steps is that one tiny key detail or ingredient needed without which implementation is difficult. Saying, "I know" to stop someone from going over the preliminaries or introductory step-by-step point has later on caused stress. When you say, "I know", in an attempt for them to skip certain steps, they stop and skip the basics, unfortunately they invariably skip the 'basics' pertaining to the concept/topic being explained to you. Later down the road, we are miserable and sad because we can't figure things out.

Patience. Develop patience. Be still and know – You. Basically, most things in life and technology start

the same way... then added on is the new point or spice. 60-90% is the same --romance, 9% is dung, and 1% is orgasm ...(village stats!). If you want the big O all the time, you miss the energy and nuances of the know-how and you will need to develop extraterrestrial mental abilities. The 'know how' is what will accelerate your genius.

Everything that is hot eventually becomes cold. Change is the way of Nature! *The old woman in a desperate attempt to kill the bed bugs that had infested her bamboo bed poured scalding hot water over the bed. The baby bugs cried out to Mama Bug, "Mama, we are going to die, we are going to die." Mama Bug coached her kids, "Hang in tight, hang in tight; everything that is hot eventually becomes cold" (Cameroonian fable).*

Understand the rhythms and cycles in all you do; it will help you plan or sit tight and wait (actively).

Understand energy, sex, and intimacy. This helps you in the transmutation of energy to be creative and joyful, else we might be preoccupied with 'junk' thoughts and can't be creative. Example is the man from Baltimore discussed earlier whose marital problems caused him to have an energy drain leading to lost property.

Engage often in dancing, deep breathing, massage, exercises, and stretching. Improved blood circulation and generated endorphins will increase your happiness. This will add more years to your life and give you a youthful look! Also, join the Entrée and Dance Club at http://entreeanddanceclub.com and get the tools to rejuvenate yourself, and knowledge of the ancient masters to create at higher levels.

Walk in the rain; sit in the rain. Go to the beach; talk to the water. Natural elements are adaptogens - fixing was necessary.

Imagine it, plan it, and do it. Action again! Action takes our mind off a 'pity me' state and directs our energy towards productivity leading to contentment.

Pay attention to the "Non-Vision" VISION Board: Here is one of my newsletters explaining what this means:

The "Non-Vision" VISION Board.

Almost everyone has heard of a vision board. What is a vision board? A vision board is the visual representation or collection of the things that we want to have, be, or do in our life. On a board, wall, or refrigerator we put cutout pictures, drawings, and/or writings of the things that we want manifested in our life, relationships, business, etc. on it. We do this to activate the law of attraction so it pulls these things from some ethereal place into our environment to enable the realization of our dreams. The idea here is that when we select these pictures and writings that charge our emotions with feelings of passion, we will begin to see those things come into our life.

Vision boards have been proven to work. What I want to talk to you about, in this newsletter, is that I found out that you do not have to be *conscious* of your vision board images for it to come to fruition. What do I mean by that? Some of us... yours truly included, have "non-intentional" vision boards. Meaning that, somewhere we have created a vision board consciously, cut pictures, words, etc. and placed them on this board and we look at this often and 'know' in our mind "this is my vision board." However, non-'intentional' vision cutouts are all over the house... still vibrating with their own natural

46

energy, whether we are aware or not of them.

What I found out is that things come true in my life that are not intentionally on the "Vision Board", which I am setting my mind on. For example, say my vision board is in the kitchen. However, I have other pictures and words in other places around the house, car, and office. Periodically, something happens in my life and later I find that picture or word was 'non intentional' somewhere around. Now that is why I title this newsletter, "the non-vision Vision Board." You can also call it, "the non-intentional Vision Board."

Years ago, a friend and I went to the Chesapeake Bay very early in the morning to watch the sun rise. It was almost an hour's drive and on our way, I saw some very nice houses with lots of glass windows. As my friend drove, I took pictures through the window. I later printed the pictures of that sunrise and put them up and also of one of the houses I really liked. Later, I moved houses and four years after being in my 'new home' I found the picture I had packed away; guess what? My "new home" had lots of glass windows. I did not consciously put this house on my Vision Board... that type of a house was for the movers and shakers in my mind - so I thought! But it happened!

In the late eighties I worked at the Ritz Carlton. Last year, I found a picture of me at one of the employee parties looking all "slim" and 'branchée' ('hot' in French --I guess). So I put this picture up on the refrigerator… "memory is our hope for the future" quote from Love Under the Kola Nut Tree. (At least I can dream...right?)

Now, I am in this picture with one of the top chefs. But when I put this picture up, I slid the portrait of him under another poster, as I was interested in remembering how slim (tiny) I used to be! Recently, men who look like this chef have contacted me for different reasons! Bingo! This solidified my non-vision Vision Board reality. Even though his image is hidden under another picture, the vibration is still at work! Something I have known for years...now I see evidence!

How can you use this information? - (Travaux Pratiques Practical Application)

Look around your house, life, and relationships. Are there ("innocent") pictures, words, drawings, and writings? Examine your life and see if you see these images playing. For example, I have coached women (and men) who say they want to be in a relationship. When you go to their house, they have only pictures of single gorgeous women on their walls...alone or with child! There are no pictures of females and males together. Replace these pictures and paintings with partnered pictures - happy ones too, please. ☺

Do you have pictures of sumptuous dishes, parties and you find yourself cooking a lot or being where there is lots of food, or being given food a lot? Choose the energy you want to activate. There is no good or bad...just what you want to activate. Do you watch TV sitcoms with scenes you consciously know you do not want in your life...however, you find your life and language like that sitcom? That is the "non-vision, vision board." I have friends who talk about dogs or cats most (all) of the time... yes they have pictures of cats on their desk, car, frig, etc. There are many other examples but for now:

- Go around your house, car, and office desk and remove images, words that vibrate contrary energy/achievement into your life that you did not intend for them to.

- In your relationship with yourself and partners, create a new vision, with mental and physical pictures of your desires.

- Use a 'new language'.

- Remember that the "non-vision" Vision Board is as active as your conscious 'vision' Vision Board. The laws of nature and the universe are constantly doing their thing, so align with them.

Remember: Words, pictures, and thoughts are all alive and working! Hmmm!

Strive To Be Happy. Powerful Tools On How To

Sleep with lights out to get a good night's sleep and a rested body to aid optimal performance and health. Melatonin is a hormone found naturally in the body, secreted by the pineal gland in the brain. When it is dark, your body produces more melatonin and less in light. Among its many benefits, melatonin is a very powerful antioxidant, and it also helps you fall asleep. Thus darkness to behold as in an African village is a very good thing (in years past, cancer was unknown in villagers, now modern conveniences channel in more diseases.) No blinking lights from things like stereos either; cover them with a cloth at night.

 Start by smiling, even if you are alone practice. One of the most powerful good energy generating tools is a smile: "A man without a smiling face must not open a shop" – Chinese proverb. Substitute "open a shop" with whatever you are trying to do, "start a relationship", "work in the service industry", "get on stage", "teach/preach..." (For example, "A man/woman without a smiling face must not start a relationship.").

Think about the effect your demeanor or sadness has on those around you. I have been privileged to sojourn with interesting characters, and in some cases when the 'emotional tyrant', be it female or male head of household returned, even the dogs retreated to their corner or rooms. Smiles, laughter, playfulness vanished from the compound. Sometimes for days! If you want happiness, inflict it on others; it will be reflected back to you. Choose to bring light instead of darkness every time you return home to your loved ones, who are missing you anxiously.

Prioritize and schedule. (I received this in a dream and I am going to share it with you. Try it; as being organized alone will

49

© 2014 Esther Lamnyam

relieve mental congestion, bring clarity, and subsequent happiness.)

Know what you are crying about... when we examine our desires for needlepoint clarity the illusion is exposed. We move on to what really matters. Truth helps.

Have a reason, a "why," to anchor your aspirations and pull you forward. This keeps you excited.

Know your power. We are so strong; we are built strong to last many, many years. Not knowing our own power creates false beliefs and being controlled by others to our disadvantage. A good example is the Harry Potter house elf, Dobby. He is actually stronger than his very powerful master! He just needs a gift of a sock for the tables to turn. Maybe knowing your inherent religion or primordial blue print will show you the 'gift' you already have.

Deal with subtle threats and mind manipulators, as they keep us very unhappy, as in the example below, which happens to be a difficult case considering the relationships:

Sophia recounting: "Many years ago, a father I know used to threaten his children with death...his! "I will die if you guys don't do XYZ".

Another father said, "Je vais boire de l'alcool dans la matinée. Sinon, si je meurs, vous allez le regretter. Donnez-moi un verre maintenant." (Translated: "I will drink liquor in the morning. Else if I die you will regret it. Give me a drink now.") He drank liquor upon waking up, threatened his kids with their distress and suffering as well as his death if they kept trying to stop him from drinking!

50

In both cases, the kids somersaulted financially, mentally, and emotionally to keep these dads alive. Basically they catered to their own abuse and what not. One of the kids called me in distress regarding the behavior and I had the occasion to be threatened by these dads (the issues that friends have can become yours!); unfortunately for them I was going through my own crisis and had not taken my being rational or being a sucker for abuse pill!

So I told them lovingly, "really! You are going to die? You know, we all will die oh... hm! Even Jesus died. Even the guys Jesus and his disciples rose from the dead died. So good for you that you are being proactive and are thinking about it. My only request is that you leave some money for your kids to bury you decently. Tell them, as it will be helpful, where all your real estate property is, what to do with XYZ, and what you want to be buried/dressed in. You know how broke, 'stupid', and 'irresponsible' your kids are; you know all those adjectives you have used on them, so make plans if you want a decent burial. Drink all you want since the kids can't stop you and you are conscious of what you are doing."

They were quiet after I said this. I had no anger or sarcasm in my voice, just presence. Then I changed the topic to something else and asked what they wanted to do that day so I made it happen. Guess what? In both cases those dads stopped the verbal, emotional, and psychological torture of their kids, and whipping the cane of death over their heads and backsides, as well as their excessive drinking. Their health is great and they are laughing and playing often with their grandkids. I did not tell the kids about this discussion, but they look at me with happy yet questioning eyes," Sophia concluded.

51

(Point: −save the dignity and honor of people you help by covering them through such attributes as, privacy, and letting bygones be bygones. Not all needs to be told, just serve, and bring happiness to all.)

Lesson: Figure out a lesson and tool here:

_____

Do you want to be healed? Do you want to be happy or is it benefiting you in some form? Why spread the suffering to folks with their own issues? This journey is hard enough for each one of us. Bear the burden of another and not put your burden on another.

Thus if you let people manipulate you for any reason they grow stronger in their abuse!

List people who are overbearing in your life now:

_____
_____
_____

How do you plan to manage this situation?

_____
_____
_____

When?

_____

Why have you not managed it before?

_____

Why Now?

_____

How would you lovingly stand your ground when they resist...and resist they will?

_____

What part did you play in creating this behavior?

_____

How will you manage that part of you now?

_____

Add more questions and answer them.

Have faith in something... something worth having faith in. Believe in a deity... this leads to a consciousness shift that will sustain you in times of battle. **Use aspects of the Bible as a self-help tool**.

     There are many self-help books are out there, most of the time only one to two key points from a great book will tide us over in our current issue. They have concepts and have awesome tools to aid in our happy journey on this earthly plane. The key is you have to try them sincerely.

Even if it is psychological, having some mighty deity to go to, or run to help us move forward. It also gives us solace when we meet not so nice people. The shelter of his or her love and protection is a fortress of peace.

Example: Sophia reminiscing: "Many years ago I worked in a very happy office. We had a great boss who knew how to manage both projects and human *beings*! Then our magic maker boss quit, as others needed his ability to create success. Guess what? We got a real magic maker boss. A woman who played with a deck of cards we had no clue about. People started getting sick, relatives died, people who could started working from home to avoid her, and husbands stopped making love to their wives. Wives started having divorce discussions and crying all day at work. What did I do? I ran to my Dad. I used to stay on my knees for a while before coming to work (praying).

One day I became wise and I realized that, though intercessory prayer is one of the most potent forms of prayers, they (coworkers) had to pray for themselves (if someone is not receptive or wanting change, your well-meant prayers (aka thoughts) will meet a stone wall and die off); so I went to everyone's desk and asked if they believed in something. There were more than fifteen nationalities on that project. I learnt a very BIG lesson. I already knew there are many gods but did not know how practical they still are today. Almost everyone had a different god they believed in and worshiped. Some had multiple gods and when we played Powerball as a group they told us they had a different god for money! Live and learn!

I remember distinctly one gentleman who had his daughter's picture at his desk and when I asked him what he believed in, he told me in a 'matter of fact way' that he believed in his six year old daughter! So I told him in a 'matter of fact way' to pray to her for the help we needed (what do I know in this vast universe?). He said he would! We needed all the resources to work and stay sane!

This particular gentleman hated this boss's tactics and made it clear to her and all in no uncertain terms. He said she could not even stand in the shadow of his beautiful, vivacious wife's butt and used other "male languages", and jokes. He played right up her alley and of course the boss reciprocated well. She had the power to make his job and life miserable, and she did. She thoroughly enjoyed doing this to the point some of us used to hurriedly finish our work to go help him with the load she levied on him.

Never try to box with a boxer when you have no clue about boxing! Never fight losing battles; bow out and walk away, then when you turn the corner, RUN; run for your life and the lives of your kids, wife, and family, and your sanity! Hello!

I cannot attribute this to any obvious reason… but his wife got sick and no doctor in the U.S. could save her… she suffered long before transitioning. I had long left the place and when I received the call about her departure from this plane, my spirit always queried me about this encounter." Sophia concluded sipping more tea.

What if his god had not been his little daughter? Maybe, just maybe, he could have been able to beat the god of the boss and the stress and negative energy absorbed and passed over to others like his wife. (Women by default are healers, but most of them do not have the technique Master Jesus had of sending negative energy into swine or mud, etc., so the energy might be too strong for them and give them headaches) (Read in "Love Under the Kola Nut Tree. What City Moms Didn't Tell You About Creating Fulfilling Relationships" about how to deal with evil people… very simple techniques, which actually work! Read therein the story of the girl and the snake. There is an antidote to everything under the sun… find it and use it)

Lessons: If you want to be happy:

- Believe in something or someone who can come to bat for you when the going gets tough. Develop a strong relationship with that something or someone.
- Call on that something or someone often and lay your case and do your part.
- Do not fight losing battles.
- Watch your mouth!
- Do not fight evil. Love is the biggest and most consistently effective antidote. Resist evil; let it dissolve or dissipate. It is always on a journey.
- Conquer your ego so you can use the tools, especially to be able to use the love tool.
- Even when you have the physical power, the spiritual power always wins. Know your spiritual side and grow with it.
- Run… run away… move out of the city… move out of town… move out of state… move out of the country. Put on your sports shoes and run. Do not look back!
- If you are smart, NEVER fight with an evil woman; not even "god is ripe enough" to mess with an evil woman. Imitate the prophet Elijah… run. If one of the greatest prophets of all time could run away from an evil woman, who are you not to? Do not let any pastor fool you with faith words, etc.; they run also! If you wear sandals, when you run to the edge of the city, remove the sandals and click off the dust of the 'place.'! God knew the deal, He just told the broken Elijah to start preparing his successor!
- Know your limits… if the boss wants you to copy that file from directory A to directory B, then from directory

56

B to directory A twenty five times, do it; get paid on Friday!

- Then, find a worthwhile course outside your work and use your talents and energy there. Know why you are working. Serve where you are allowed to serve, else you will be sick and may become demented. Find your purpose and live it outside of 'work'.

- Don't worry about the esthetics. When I left college and started working, I believed I could change the world! (You know how the endocrine system works us, especially at that age.) My questions, suggestions, and fixes on that job antagonized others, and I woke up to reality one day when I wrote a computer program that I considered a monumental task. During my presentation of the program, right on my Landing Page of the compiled program, the big bosses spent time complaining and arguing about the fonts and colors I had used! I could not believe what these greats were focusing on!!! I kept trying to bring them back to the data that was going to be used at that highest echelon but, no, they would not get past the font and color (my first time hearing about Barney… some colors reminded them of Barney!). My Ego boiled, anger smiled at me and as I was about to mentally think something bad about these people I had the highest regard for, a higher voice said 'calm down, calm down, now you know." I listened! From that time on I never focused on the esthetics because they will ALWAYS be changed. Sometimes legitimately, sometimes because the boss needs to put his presence on the project. Don't fight losing battles please. You will take this home and upset your family… they need your presence… stay sane and happy!

57

- Add your own lessons learned:
- _____
- _____
- _____
- RUN! Seriously!

Remember. "Memory is our hope for the future" is a quote from Love Under the Kola Nut Tree. You have certainly had bigger issues in the past. Draw back on the resolutions and know this is a journey and sometimes the road might be rocky or swampy but you are programmed to go through it already. Enjoy the troubleshooting! That is where the gold is!

The heart forgets! If not, the raw grief of dead loved ones and broken relationships will kill us! This muscle, instead of keeping sad memories lets them go and keeps memories of love. Renew. Don't go pull from the trash what was vomited. Help the heart forget so happiness is ushered in.

Be courageous and strong. You already have courage and strength coded in you. It will help you stand up for you, stand up to bullies, and stand up for your cause.

Bottom line is, do YOU want to be happy and joyful? When the Master and Teacher, Jesus, helped people he usually asked them if they wanted it. Or they somehow indicated they wanted it. If you do not want to be healed, all these self-help tools will be for naught!

No one can inflict joy on you and succeed without you being receptive. Things like swallowing, excreting, getting an orgasm, joyfulness, and being happy can only be brought into manifestation by you. Contract the right muscles by yourself and create the atmosphere you desire.

Example by folktale: There are certain things only you can do for yourself: There was a very rich father who had a son. He had lots of property, wealth, and servants. His first son was not just spoilt; he was a lazy kid and became a lazy youth and grew to a lazy man. It was easy for him to get away with being lazy because either his mom or dad would eventually get a servant to submit to his wishes.

He eventually got married. (You see issues… already too?). The wedding of course was the talk of the land and went on for days.

He lived happily with his bride. However, the father became disillusioned. He and his wife wanted grandkids badly. Maybe they knew their heritage would not go on if this lazy boy were to be left in charge.

As the months and years went by and no grandchild was forth coming, I suspect he talked to his daughter in law and asked some questions… so this is when he came to his son and said,

"Son, I love you so much, from the time you were a tiny, tiny baby in your mother's arms, suckling from her breast, I have provide you with everything a father can for a child under the sun. I have educated you, built you a house, and married you a wife. But son, there are certain things I cannot do for you which only you can do. You have to get me a grandson. You have to go into your wife; only you can do that and get your mother and I a grandchild for our old age."

Thus, there are certain things only YOU can do. Even the most loving dad will not make your love making for YOU. He cannot make your JOY for you. It is within you. The foundation is laid, the table set, the guest invited… but only you can, from within, use these tools to do the rest.

(I heard this folktale as a kid; now as a self-growth coach, cases I listen to, show me this is happening today! Yes, people are that lazy! Living with any? Get them coached to learn how to awaken their energy and the fire that lies within.)

Plan. Plan your life. Plan your day. Plan your menu. Plan even 'little' things. Planning and working your plan makes a big difference in how your countenance will end up looking. Many times we are not happy because we did not plan well. I discovered when I played soccer that there are always other travelers on the road, no matter the time.

"Where are all these people going to at this early or late hour?" I would ask and think they are also asking the same questions. If I did not plan right, I was going to be late or not get there at all as in one situation. The stress of being late got me more stressed. This is just one example; but planning can be for something as simple as which route to take, where to go for dinner, what time to leave for the airport. Sometimes you have to calculate backwards, as in the example of when to get to the airport for a flight. Three to five minutes of thinking through beforehand saves tons of stress, money, and keeps you and your associates happy!

Planning the week or day the night before can save you headaches. Having ALL your ducks in row... even printed material the night before will save you unhappiness and stress. Know your part in the program and when you come online or on stage. So in case of any eventuality, you have very little to worry about except the event that popped up. This point alone has caused much grief. It takes a while to rebuild relationships, if at all, depending on how nature and humans are spinning!

Touching base with all involved and even mapping a time line will save you frustration and also help others. Take a leadership role, even if with subtlety by helping the leader with helpful suggestions. This will eliminate the "I thought, I thought you or X had to do XYZ...."

61

Speak or forever forget your angry thoughts. Ask questions. Ask clearly. Good questions have the answers within; it is like recursive magic. We all keep learning to ask clear questions.

Do not assume what people mean. If you are not clear or you heard from a third party, ask for clarification. Do not assume they know your wishes or that you are baffled. This is a red feather in my hat; it can save your money, relationships, health, and more.

Example: Let's use a female as an example to explain this; (not picking on women) she would say, to her partner that she is stressed about or angry with, "he is a man, he should know…"

It is good to point out that neither men nor women are psychics or prophets that can read your mind. And most mind readers are challenged regarding relationships anyway. If you want your partner to know your wishes, speak them clearly. Ask or speak and it shall be known!

Example of how thinking and coming to false conclusions without your partner being consulted can cause issues.

This story keeps begging me to tell it:

1. Tom and Silence: Many, many years ago, a friend of mine took me out of town to meet his family. We spent time with his family and he took me around the 'village' to meet his friends, old school mates, and retired military friends. The part of the story that helps to make the point above is this: on our way back to town we stopped at a WAWA convenience store and got some gas and sandwiches. As we continued on our journey, at some point, I noticed our conversation had died down.

Let me call this friend Tom. Tom who had been wooing me, telling me great stories, and jokes stopped talking. I realized Tom was no longer interested in talking and just focused on driving the car. What did I do? In my mind I started conjuring all the reasons he had stopped talking. All of them negative. "Oh, he only wanted me to help him clean his mama's house; he was interested in winning points for himself by showing me off; he needed companionship for this long trip that is why he took me. He was not really ever interested in me." All these joy-killing thoughts flooded my mine and I conjured more thoughts as to how he was not even doing XYZ for me.

See the pattern? Negative thoughts called on to more negative thoughts to the point that we are ready to break up with our partners verbally, as we have already done so mentally with all these negative conclusions in our head.

In the past I would have just said bye-bye and not given him the benefit of the doubt. The more I thought these thoughts it seemed to me it was a physical conversation with him so he knew my thoughts...in *my* mind!

However, this experience happened at a time in my life when I had grown in courage and relationship building skills to asking questions first before jumping to conclusions. So I mustered up the courage and glanced over to my left at him. Faking a calm demeanor, I asked the dreaded question as I was convinced he was going to tell me some not too nice stuff about my visit with his family and the relationship, "What's up Tom; you've been so quiet for a while now. Anything I need to know?"

Bracing myself for his 'obvious' response… ready to burst into a tirade of words and tears at his response. He responded,

"Dang, I have been trying to get this piece of meat out of my teeth. The dang thing seems to be stuck."

As he moved his left arm into my view, I saw he had a dental floss on his hand with which he had been flossing while he drove the car with his right hand and I was seated in the passenger seat to his right. Off course he could not carry on a conversation while doing this.

I sunk into my seat in mental embarrassment. How many times had I broken out of relationships in general without asking questions, jumping to assumptions and making horrible choices; and I am embarrassed to say, conclusions about innocent people without giving them the chance to explain! From then on, I have asked questions and encouraged others to do so as well.

2. Tip via humor: The man with an unsatisfied-able wife: My friend, Dr. Morgan, told me this joke many years ago in the eighties but it is still funny, I chuckle to myself always when I recall it. How true it is still today! A man married a very beautiful woman that he loved very much. He dedicated his mind, body, and wealth to her. She stayed home while he went to work. Every day when he returned home, she met him expectantly at the door. She would give him kisses, and take his brief case from his hand. As he walked into the house, she would inspect him thoroughly, prying over his suit and body.

When she found hair on his suit, she picked up the hair, observed it and busted out crying. "Oh it was a blond this time." No matter how much the man denied it, saying he was not with a blond did not console her.

The next day the same scenario occurred and she found hair again.

"Oh, it was a brunette this time," and she busted out crying. This went on for a long time and the husband did not know what to do, as she always managed to find some hair on his clothing.

Every day it was a different hair color leading thus to sobbing, wailing, and sulking.

One day as usual, she met him at the door, gave him loving sweet kisses, took his briefcase from him, and proceeded to inspect his suit. However, this time, she found nothing on his jacket.

Guess what… ah ha, she busted out crying again!!

"What now," the stunned and perplexed husband asked. "You found no hair on me this time, why are you crying?"

"Even bald ones too?!!" she sobbed.

Hehehehe!

If you look for trouble, you will find trouble! Unfortunately for most of us, trouble drives out happiness!

Practical Application:

What lessons have you learned from this story?

_____ .

_____

_____

There is a big difference between a narrative and a supplication. This bears emphasis - if you need a service, favor, or money from someone, do not simply tell them a story about your situation or plan and *in your mind* conclude that was a request for money from them or their help. Actually make the request clearly known!

This point is a source of heartache and unhappiness for many. It is true that cultures defer and many cultures are too "sensitive" to "ask", "beg", or supplicate. However, spiritual principles are not culture specific. It (Bible) says, "ask and it shall be given to you."   (A new rule, is to, "give, and it will be given to you.")

Practical Application Example of, "tell your sorry story and it shall be given to you." This issue causes so much unhappiness, as in the case of Rose, a friend and sister:

So Rose calls me in major distress, which is very untypical for her,
        "What is up Niet?" I ask. Niet is the name we call each other.

"I am on my way to see you, I need to cry on your shoulder!" she replies and hangs up.

There goes my afternoon! After my aunt Maya Sophia, the queen, left back to Africa, she seemed to have bestowed on me some of her Maya wisdom as my friends and others were always asking for feedback. Well giving feedback is not bad... what scared me is that they took my feedback seriously and implemented it. So I started being really careful about what I said... not easy when you want to chew someone up!

Rose tells me this story about her dad and brother, a story I have heard from many and experienced. In one case, her brother calls her and tells her how he wants to travel across the country to visit a friend. Only issue is that he has no money. She sends him money and he loved the heck out of her, and blessed her.

One day he calls again. He has found him a fine woman. If he does not marry her, he will die! He needs money to get an apartment worthy of such a chick. "Oh, I am so lucky!" He talks about this fine goddess incessantly and is so full of joy. Rose is very happy for her little brother and yes you guessed right; she sends lots of money and more than he needs for the apartment. She loves him and she has money. This went on for years.

Another time the brother told her he intended to start a business. He told her how much such a business gets started for and how lucrative it was, and he would be making lots of money; that is, if only he had the capital to start the business. Rose was traveling and did not send money and forgot because she was very busy as a lawyer. Her brother called weeks later angry and accused her of not giving him the money he asked her for. He told her how he missed a big business opportunity because *he asked her for money,* but she refused.

67

I sat and listened to Rose, who was telling me this and I am still waiting for her point because I have heard similar stories. Bear with me. So Rose continued her narrative still very distressed.

Another day the brother "asked" (story) her for money and this time Rose was having financial issues with her firm and other personal issues. So she says to her brother "I sent you lots of money, what did you do with it? I always send you money for this and that, what is your problem that you cannot handle this and keep calling me." Know what her brother replied to her?

"I never asked you for money. Why do you give us money and curse us over it." She had heard this before from her dad, but this time she got it! (I recalled many others telling me the same story with weary!)

She finally realized at no point did any of them consciously "ask" her for money. They told a *story* of their plans and issues, and she financed them. However, if once in a while she did not, they then claimed they had "asked" her for money and she refused even though all they did was "tell" her their plans and needs.

At no point did they claim ownership or show reverence. She was darned if she gave; she was darned if she did not.

Rose realized she had been bamboozled in a way. He refused to take ownership to "asking" her directly, thereby honoring her hard work and also owning to the fact that he needed to step up to the plate. If she complained about what he did with the money, he took offense as his irresponsibility was being exposed. When life started hitting her hard, as it will eventually do to all of us as we age, she realized the tactics and how she had by unknowing using another principle of "bear ye the

68

burdens of one another," enabled laziness, abuse, non-reverence, and more.

Sitting with me, both she and I realized we had some hard decisions to make. Was the fault that of our families, culture, love or ours?

As parents or people who have more, when we try to make life easy for our kids and siblings and other family members we unintentionally violate spiritual principles. We also take away their muscle to be creative to come up with self-help tools. Later on in life, they take this "tell and it shall be given to me" mentality to their jobs and relationships, and when it blows up in their faces it creates havoc for many! When I watch Nature channels on TV, the baby animals are taught and then encouraged or forced to learn to feign for themselves. This serves all involved later!

Even if you are going to give, teach people holistically to ask. Spiritual principles do not care about our egos or cultures! Jesus used story telling or parables to be able to give without them asking; covering them in a way.

If you get nothing from this little book but just this point, it will give you and the future generation much joy and happiness for the rest of your life and of those you interact with! First steps will be very hard, both for the donor and the perpetual recipient! (Hang in tight.)

Lessons Learned and Your Action Points:

_____.

_____.

_____.

- Know thyself: Self-knowledge will help bring you joy. Set Boundaries. People will always come to the edge of any boundary you set; if not set, they will be inside your life, house, finances, relationships, business, etc.
- Teach others how to fish for themselves. Do not be a fisherman for everyone. It might kill you! Worst of all, it will disable their learning and set them up for failure later and painful relationships. Learn from the animals.
- Culture is not always correct, nor the colonies and kingdoms which may have now dissolved. If associated with multiple cultures, choose what culture's norms to go with and modulate the cultures as appropriate, else by being "bi-cultural" you might end up "bi-polar."

Believe what people tell you about them! I can't stress this enough. In today's world, it is almost impossible to properly vet people we have dealings with. However, you can begin to know who people are through the daily mundane, so to speak, stories they share or volunteer. They know themselves. Don't say, "No, you do not mean that!" They do! A man of very high stance once told a bunch of us in the buzzing of a networking happy hour, "Oh me, I lie a lot". My spirit told me to believe him. Others thought he was being a joker as usual. Later we found out that most of what people knew about him was false!

If a guy tells you, "I like football," believe him and accept him and give him space to enjoy his games! Change that and he changes to a different creature than the one you connected with. Bye, bye. He is not going to change for you (maybe while in your presence, hehehe). If a woman says she likes lots of shoes and money, believe her; go in knowing the deal. Don't act surprised

70

later and try to change the person, thus leading to fights, quarrels, and more unhappy stuff.

Train your mind to dwell on the essentials. As seen in the example with Tom above, the mind is a whole world loaded with characters and scripts; if we leave it on its own, there is no telling where it will lead us if we are not at the reigns consciously.

Prophesize unto thyself great and good things - daily. Be your own best advocate. Again, talk out loud and tell the invisible energies to help bring into fruition what serves you and your purpose. You never know... it might work... it does work.

71

Practical Application by example:

1. In the nineties, I moved into a home vacated by a public figure. I loved the place and so did my friends. I strive to be a happy-go-stay-constructive person. However, one day it came to my realization that for a few weeks, every evening, after having returned home from work, I felt down, sad, and lost, not being productive or alert. It was so powerful I could feel it and I could not explain, yet it was so subtle it was hard to make a fuss about it. Like a hide and seek game. The day I finally realized this had been happening consistently, I got up and started talking out loud in the house. I was not being productive and at this moment did not care who heard me or thought I had finally lost my mind. I told whatever spirit, energy, laziness, procrastination, etc. that was in my presence to go to its mama, as it was not welcomed chez moi. It had no permission in my space. I think I had read to do this somewhere. That evening, that spirit of nonchalance and depression went bye-bye, so to speak.

2. Years ago, I started a job near a major train station stop. I walked through that train station daily in the morning and evening. After some time, I observed that my knees hurt in the mornings as I walked through this station. I thought it was just coincidence. But when it happened often around the same spot, I told one of my coworkers in the office.

    "Paul, this might sound weird and spooky, but it seems my knees hurt when I walk through this train station some mornings …like someone bites or pinches them." I told him this expecting him to laugh and ridicule me. However, he said to me,

"You too, I have the same experience! Don't you see me moseying in here most mornings with my knees killing me? "He responded. Hmmmm!

"You know what?" I said, "let's start talking or singing when we walk through there."

"I am with you," he replied; "I'll try anything." When he said that, I knew this was really a serious thing I had observed. I planned to speak out loud the next day when I experienced the pain again.

Off course when we do not have an issue we forget; it did not happen so I forgot about my plan. But guess what... a week later, in the morning, I was happily singing my way to work and I felt a "bite" in my knee around the same area in that train station. I thought, "Too bad for you... I am armed... with words." I started talking to my knees and to whatever pain or 'biting' energy was around.

"Knee, be strong, oh. Don't fail me, oh. I took care of you, gave you some breakfast, vitamins, and minerals. I have done my part. We are partners. Be strong and nice to me. You are healthy, etc." Breathe in deep and blow out.

"Whatever energy is messing with my knee, leave me alone. We have nothing for or against you. I need my knees in good form." Well I just made up stuff and spoke and the knee pain went away. It happened periodically and I kept speaking to my knee and the ethers. (Yes, that was me speaking out loud ☺) Eventually it stopped happening. I only remember now as I search for examples and tools to serve you.

In my book "Love Under the Kola Nut Tree. What City Moms Didn't Tell You About Creating Fulfilling Relationships," Maya Sophia teaches us that elements in the universe are alive and active whether we know it or not. Knowledge helps us do your part and lose frustration and un-happiness.

Make others happy. "Happiness, love, and peace are perfumes you cannot pour on others without getting a few drops on yourself."

Keep your cheerleaders! Even God says praise me!

Example: When Johan was an up and coming young man, he had a hard time finding long lasting jobs and relationships. He finally found a girl that stuck with him. His girlfriend believed in him and she 'helped mate' him, encouraging him and making sure he ate well in all dimensions. All he had to focus on was work and climbing Uncle Sam's ladder (instead of Jacob's ladder!).

After he got to the top, he socialized with women who dressed like you see in fashion catalogues. His girl was unaware she was not measuring up until she was given the boot. She cried, but she knew her abilities and herself. She also knew how much she had put into Johan and how the boy needed fire under his behind, even though he did not know it. Less than a year after she was sacked from her girlfriend position, Johan started falling apart. Not only did his job fade out of his hands, his health and polished look did also. She had been the cheerleader and engineer in the background. His evil did not live after him it lived within him; it was too late to repent.

If you are going to give up your cheerleader, man, or woman who was your support in formative years, do it in a holistic way!! Chapters can be written just on this point. There is

74

the intersection of the physical and spiritual. The spiritual always wins. Most of us are carried through success by other's spiritual energy exerted to cover us. Do not let go of your cheerleaders, especially those in your 'baby' years! (I have seen men who dropped stay at home wives or supposedly "uneducated" wives after success and their lives plummeted or flat lined no matter how hard they pushed up!)

Accusations bring a lot of unhappiness. Find ways to ask for others' stories, nicely. Many marriages have broken up – irretrievably because of accusations. Whether true or false, even a thief does not like to be accused... they plead "not-guilty", even when caught red handed – go figure! To lay aside the ego is tough for the majority of us, but do not wakeup a sleeping dragon.

For example, Joshua tells Mariyah this story: He has known Michelle for years, but this year, the relationship starts moving into a potential "go steady" zone. He is really excited about this, as he thinks Michelle is the type of girl he might sync his "potential partner thoughts" into. He looks forward to knowing her more intimately instead of the casual dinner hour with other folks or group activities.

Michelle invites Joshua for dinner to meet her old school friends and family coming to town, thus setting the initial stage for this relationship metamorphosis.

Joshua is looking forward to this and gets to the dinner on time, but it takes another hour half for the folks to start trickling in. Joshua comments on the time and finds out Michelle gave him an earlier time for dinner than she gave others. He is not happy about this but keeps his mouth shut, as he is now very hungry. During the dinner, which he enjoys, he listens, and comments, and observes.

75

A few days later he meets with Michelle, unaware that magma is about to erupt. She accuses him of being too quiet during dinner because he was pissed off with her about the wrong time she had given him.

"Listen Mariyah," he tells me. "At no time was I upset after the original time clarification. I really enjoyed my dinner. I listened and mostly commented because the family was talking a lot due to the excitement of the kids and grownups meeting after a while."

"From what you explained, Michelle says you were upset because she gave you the wrong time and you had to wait an hour and a half even before being seated. What do you make of that?" Mariyah asks. Joshua explained that once he realized the deal, he settled into the new time and zoned out, as hunger kept his energy very low.

"What about the accusation you were not being talkative at dinner because you were upset with Michelle?" Mariyah asks.

That is when Joshua becomes really distressed and explains that, due to his religion, he had been on a forty day fast and was three weeks into the fast. Knowing he would be at dinner that night, he had broken fast at home with a broth. Dinner being late, and having not eaten all day, forced him to conserve even more energy by being calm (mistaken for anger towards Michelle). The family had too many stories to tell so he enjoyed listening and chiming in as needed (again mistaken by Michelle as anger for the time play she did).

Her continuous accusations forced him to disclose to her he had been fasting and more about his spirituality, something very intimate to him. He only pulled this religious card out because he was falling in love with Michelle and she was relentless about putting blame on him. Yet she pulled out another accusation and never once sympathized with his dilemma, nor commented on his spirituality. She even resorted to using tears to get him to beg her not to be angry with him. Then she resorted to blaming her childhood mama and dad

76

issues for her life now.

In the following days, he realized that Michelle was not the girl for him; and though being slammed hard by Michelle he was happy the incident happened. Her accusations, conclusions, and wanting to be begged, even when she had clearly given him the false time for dinner, made him realize that we do not really know people until we try to inch in closer into their world.

Lessons:

- Not all that looks like a done deal is a done deal.

- Don't be surprised when those we love kick us hard… where it hurts!

- If your religion is very important to you and someone's religious affiliation is different from yours, discuss that upfront before investing your time and emotions into a potential mate.

-If you have to be the one begging all the time, even when you are clearly not guilty of the accusations, then think if you can live this way for the rest of your life with this person.

-People have many faces, one for work, one for personal life, one for wooing others, etc. How can you find out?

-Though Michelle and Joshua are of the same religion, they practice it differently. So, just because we are of the same religion with others does not give them a passport into our lives. Dig deeper.

-If Joshua had not been fasting, leading to his being at a very different vibratory mental state than he usually was, he would have pulled out his mobile device and distracted his mind while waiting. He also would have been very talkative and into the crazy stories during dinner, and may have completely missed the revelation that Michelle and him may not be a perfect match or that there is a lot of work to do to begin to get deeper into a relationship.

The silence and presence gained from fasting takes away your arguing and fighting energy, thus you let the chips fall where they may; situations and people then become self-evident.

77

As I explained before, the intangibles are what I have observed break down lots of relationships and bring unhappiness. Six-pack abs, long hair, fast cars, etc., fade into nothingness when we move into another zone of relationships. The physical, the emotional, and instinct pull us in, but as we move to the higher zones like mental and spiritual, these attributes are not much welcomed!

*Invest in relationship preparation, or whatever your vision is: Lay the groundwork or foundation today for your older age, which starts for most as kids and teenagers. Plan your nights in the day. Plan your evenings in the morning, your summers in winter. In the morning, I see light long before I see the sun!

Desiderata: Learn this poem by heart or read it daily. There was no television when I was growing up. What we had then was the radio. Between the ages of eight and ten or so, there was a poem that the radio station closed the day with. It is, "The Desiderata" by Max Ehrmann. I unknowingly learned it by heart... it has served me. Use it too. Give writers of inspirational works the benefit of doubt and try what they say... you will only lose frustration if their ideas work. Here below is the poem:

Desiderata - by Max Ehrmann

Go placidly amid the noise and haste, and remember what peace there may be in silence.

As far as possible, without surrender, be on good terms with all persons. Speak your truth quietly and clearly; and listen to others, even to the dull and the ignorant, they

78

too have their story. Avoid loud and aggressive persons; they are vexations to the spirit.

If you compare yourself with others, you may become vain and bitter; for always there will be greater and lesser persons than yourself. Enjoy your achievements as well as your plans. Keep interested in your own career, however humble; it is a real possession in the changing fortunes of time.

Exercise caution in your business affairs, for the world is full of trickery. But let this not blind you to what virtue there is; many persons strive for high ideals, and everywhere life is full of heroism. Be yourself. Especially, do not feign affection. Neither be cynical about love, for in the face of all aridity and disenchantment it is perennial as the grass.

Take kindly to the counsel of the years, gracefully surrendering the things of youth. Nurture strength of spirit to shield you in sudden misfortune. But do not distress yourself with imaginings. Many fears are born of fatigue and loneliness.

Beyond a wholesome discipline, be gentle with yourself. You are a child of the universe, no less than the trees and the stars; you have a right to be here. And whether or not it is clear to you, no doubt the universe is unfolding as it should.

Therefore be at peace with God, whatever you conceive Him to be, and whatever your labors and aspirations, in the noisy confusion of life, keep peace in your soul.

With all its sham, drudgery, and broken dreams, it is still a beautiful world.

Be cheerful. Strive to be happy.

Max Ehrmann c.1920

Think both inside and outside the box. There is always an easier way. There are many routes to your home and to your dreams, just keep researching. There have been times that I have gone North, to go South or Northwest. If you have the destination in mind and are open to other routes... you will find that the joy is in the journey. Excite yourself by looking for alternatives.

Give yourself time to digest a situation. Be like the Goat - swallow then chew on it later. Do not get angry and sad right away. You will lose sleep and maybe raise your blood pressure. In most cases you will find the solution and that it is not the end of the world. Thus like Maya Sophia says in Love Under the Kola Nut Tree"

She would say, "Some of these things I tell you might not make sense, but I am leaving soon and I have to tell you these things so you can improve your life and that of the generation to come. Listen, even if it does not make sense now. Be like the goat, which eats lots of grass in the daytime or in good weather then at night regurgitates and chews on it well. Meditate on these things I tell you with an open mind later and ask for Light to be poured on it for illumination."

Be like the lion. Live consciously. Go out with a mission daily. Stay home with a mission. Do not be like the cow. Read this cow-go-eat-grass mentality then cow gets slaughtered excerpt from Love Under the Kola Nut Tree about Rose's boyfriends all called Mike:

> "Then there was Mike Thompson, her resident stalker. He had what Rose called a "cow-go-eat-grass" mentality. He worked, worked out, came home, and sat still flipping through TV channels. He only got up to answer the call of nature, get something she asked for, and went right back to his couch. But he kept an eye on her, knowing where she was every minute. He would not take advantage of the free education opportunities offered by his company though he had worked there for almost two decades.
> "A cow goes out, eats grass, comes back at dusk, sleeps; goes out in the morning, eats grass, comes back at dusk, sleeps, goes out in the morning... you get the picture. No ambition, goals, initiative, or plans for next year, let alone the future. If I continue with him, very soon I would not remember why I went to school," Rose said to me."

Spend Time and Money on Yourself and Your Aspirations.
Many times people get upset because a partner, parents, or corporation has not spent money on them for whatever need such as education. Determine what you need and spend your money to get it. You will inevitably invite invisible money agents to you to help you accomplish the goal.

Example: Riyah needed a better paying position, but the company would not pay for training and neither did she have the $3000.00 to pay for the class and certification. However, she knew that if she did not make that move, she was doomed to be at a certain level for a long time, because climbing the corporate ladder would not have helped even if she did. So she went to the credit union and they gave her a loan pronto. She hunkered down and studied! Years later this training came into play in a major way! Her unhappiness would have spanned years, even a lifetime, if she had not opted for the pain of paying on the front end.

Practical Application:

1. Open an account with the credit union. With most Credit Unions you can do this with five dollars.
2. Project where you want to go with your career and take the necessary classes. Even if the position is open in your company and you are obviously next in line, Department of Labor laws may restrict the company giving it to you because you do not have the established certificate. Learn how to work with manmade laws and then integrate spiritual principles. You can blame the company, manager, color codes, etc. all you want. These are only people

appointed or hired, like you, to do a job. They also have to follow the manmade rules we have made!

3. Keep your credit clean. In America, this will carry you further than the richest dad or partner.

Have Desires in Your Heart. In Psalm 20 it says, "May He give you the desire of your heart and make all your plans succeed." Another chapter says, "Delight yourself in the Lord, and he will give you the desires of your heart." "The heart of man plans his way, but the Lord establishes his steps." The pre-requisite is thus that you have a desire and, or a plan in your heart. Sometimes we think our desires are not being granted, but they are.

Consider this, if you mentally want a higher paying job but what your heart dwells on most of the time is intimacy, you will get intimacy most of the time. Then once in a while you think about your job and say the desires of your heart (job) are not being granted. Hello! You got sex right? Or what you dwell on. Plan and align your heart with your mind and actions; do your part and watch magic happen. The laws work... all the time. Do the work! Ask another what they want, don't be surprised if they say, "I don't know." Try it! Many a times, I have to remember this tip also and most of what I am sharing with you.

Travaux Pratiques/Practical Application

1. Think about your life going forward.
2. What are all the things you would like to accomplish? List them.

3. What are the top five things if nothing else you would like to accomplish? Say the universe for five things guaranteed your success, only if you spent the rest of your life having them as your **main** focus.
4. Pick one, and for the next few weeks or months work on it using some of the principles discussed.
5. Once you get the hang of it, goal setting, doing something daily towards this goal, consistency, making it fun; then add another goal that can be done in parallel.
6. Lessons learned:

_____

_____

Learn to be with you. Know thy self. Some relationship issues can and have led to mental issues. When we do not have a center, at the root, we become very needy for companionship. So we end up suffocating another human being. This human in an attempt to survive, pulls away from us. The more they pull away the more we stick close, pout, harass, bully, control, beg, blame them, etc. If you watch nature channels on TV with animals, you will notice they all want to be alone from time to time, so too with humans.

When we have not learned to be alone with ourselves, our partners have already become victims even before the relationship starts. But is the partner really a victim? Are they looking to be needed and later get overwhelmed?

Learn to be with you and appreciate, love, give, restrict, and encourage yourself. Then observe yourself and ask,

1. Would I like to be a friend to me?
2. Would I like to date me?

84

3. Would I like to live in the same house with me?
4. Do I love me?
5. Would I recommend me as a partner to another?
6. Would I marry me?
7. Why don't I like/love me?
8. What am I running from?
9. What am I running to?
10. Am I looking outside?
11. Have I looked within ...truthfully?
12. Think about your answers to these questions on the list.
13. What would you do to be centered and discover and live your true self?

_____

_____

_____

Try it out. If there are issues, go back to the drawing board and refine.

Always look within. Close your eyes always when in an unhappy place and observe. Within you, you will find the genesis. Grieve it and correct it.

The seed is within YOU. All there is and ever will be is within. Society is just a bunch of people ...like you. Their survival makes them create rules. Society then becomes an individual! The all, is in the one, and the one, is in the all.

Let hindsight be your foresight. But if you think you have no worthwhile hindsight, then let my now wisdom hindsight be your foresight! Young people have lots of ideas and answers.

Rightly so as puberty and the endocrine system is playing a major role in their lives. They can come up with ingenious concepts and do amazing things. Call it the bravery or folly of youth sometimes. However, looking around, most of us who have tried our own methods of self-aggrandizement have not always been very successful, so let the 'elders' help you. At any stage in our lives, there is always an 'elder.' Listen to the elders, even if you really want to bulldoze your way through life. There are too many laws you are not yet aware of that might block you and many can get you a bad record. Thus, **listen to the elders…**

The technical part of the job is easy, as we eventually find out. It is managing the interconnected of all involved that is the crux of the matter. Hard as this may sound we can send someone to the moon and back. At the end of the day we can read the manual, call the manufacturer, or trash the product and get a brand new one. However, the human relationships are where the scratch is. Invest in learning how to deal with other beings. Neighbor loving helps, selflessness helps, and tips shared here therein.

Fortunately or unfortunately depending on how you look at it, after God and His mastermind group created the earth, He pulled Himself out of it and gave the reigns of dominion, creativity, and leadership to "them" (man and woman). While we are waiting on Him, he is waiting on us, as there is a clear division of labor; thus it is a partnership, each playing their part for success and joy.

Faith without taking action is like watching a movie and at the end we say, "that was a darn good movie." You have to become the actor in your own life to get

86

manifestation. If it is not working, then maybe that is not the route to take or you are missing an ingredient. If Monday, Tuesday, or Wednesday's anointing service did not work, chances are Thursday's through Sunday's and all night prayers might not work. If all night prayers worked, Africa would not be where it is today! Find the missing ingredient and give the Universe a chance to show off!

Pay the Universe; also called Satikak or Sarakak in the village. This potent point I learned from the villagers. However, it is a very Biblical principle. Any time ill is averted or you get something good, be it a job, a spouse, a baby, a serious problem somehow solved, health relief, or for supposedly no reason at all, pay the Universe. You can do this thanksgiving in the form of giving money to any one – any amount purposely given from the heart is good, help others, throw a party, community service, tithing, even feeding animals.

If you received advice paid for or not and you think you got that for a steal, do a Sarakak, even if it means just giving worthwhile feedback or comments on the page online or a testimonial. This point alone can save your health and life! If you have been having repeated health issues or repeated relationship failures, try implementing this point (with other self-growth tools!).

Even when King David was given a free threshing floor to build an altar for the LORD on, he refused. "But the king replied to Araunah, "No, I insist on paying you for it. I will not sacrifice to the LORD my God burnt offerings that cost me nothing." So David bought the threshing floor and the oxen and paid fifty shekels of silver for them." (2 Samuel 24:18-24) Many of us are victims of

87

'free stuff'. Just remember 'grounding' and that matter or energy has to be converted from one form to another, we cannot destroy it, but we need the form in our lives that will move the needle of the compass for us.

In the Bible you always see this... a celebration even after or before a war. Energy, healing, transmutations, or successes need to be grounded so our aspirations can stick... for good or for a long time. When we bind on earth, to ground our bindings (job, spouse, healings, etc.) we need to bind in heaven. (Whatever is bound on earth gets bound in heaven for the religious folks.)

Sarakak is a way to do that. Leave a tip!

Tame your ego as you grow older and as you want to succeed. I have heard many bad things being said about the ego. However, I believe all emotions or things created by God are 'good' or really 'beautiful' as in my dialect. We need to understand what they are, their place, and time in the life cycle. For example, prayer is good yet can be destructive... as in the "power of word". As prayer is basically at the machine language level *thought* or *sound of words*. How you use it is the key. So too is ego.

To make my point about ego, consider this, we do not say a child has a big ego. But most of us grownups with big egos behave exactly as kids! (Kids need to have really big egos for us to kiss, wipe their butts, and love it as well as for us to be at their beck and call. Ego in my opinion should be in an inverse proportion, as we grow older.)

88

Thus **learn to be with you. Know thy self.** When something that causes us misery is brought to light and understanding, it naturally disappears. Some things can only be conquered by light; ego is one of them. Once you go back to the dark...it will resurface...thus, choose what quadrant to stay in.

Consider this excerpt from my book "Love Under the Kola Nut Tree. What City Moms Didn't Tell You About Creating Fulfilling Relationships":

"Your final *Travaux Pratique:* Become that which you want to attract gravitates towards. Imitate nature. If you want to attract bees become a flower. If you want to attract birds become a seed. If you want to attract squirrels become nutty. If you want to attract growth, joy, beauty, brightness, and color become a light simply become the sun. If you want to attract people who laugh and joke and have fun become humorous and easy going. What you attract is a function of what you exude. It is all about you and what you bring to a relationship. As a human being, *become* daily through the alchemy of thoughts knowing that to transmute you sometimes have to use an element. For example, to make stew salt, water, and oil will not mix but the *element of* fire *(heat)* will transmute the process for you so they can combine beautifully and tastefully to *become* stew. So in your relationships, figure out the element that will help you *become* what you want, be it husband, wife, teacher, healer, lover. The *becoming* is where the beauty and joy is. BEING is God; you are a human BEING. Be.

Peace. Be Still.

Be still and know.

Be still and know you.

Be still and know you are.

Be still and know you are Man. Be still and know you are Woman.

Be.":

Do a lot of research on the front end before starting any worthwhile endeavor. Much unhappiness is brought about by not being able to get away from situations… jobs, marriages, career paths, etc. gotten into without careful analysis.

As youths, we had this mantra, "do not welcome things into your life that will be very hard to say goodbye to." Have mantras and honor them.

Go ahead and live or experience the results… mentally. As in Desiderata, dark imaginings can be very harmful. What we think about, we inevitably invite into our lives. In cases where the potential outcome is negative, pull it in quickly and shatter it. Let me explain by using this example:

A coworker of Mariyah's complained about her husband. But the complaints intensified to talks about divorce. She was sure he was planning to divorce her. As a friend, Mariyah encouraged her to not think so, but to believe and have faith in thinks working out. The faith audiotapes she had been sharing were not working for her in this situation! This went on for a while. At one point she had a mild 'seizure', aka a heart attack to the point her speech was impaired. She eventually recovered and talks of divorce continued. One day, as she complained about the same situation, Mariyah was too busy to console her. Mariyah had lots of work and deadlines to meet; and no matter what advice had been given to this woman; she did not follow through, even the therapist's suggestions. So Mariyah said to her,

"You are right, your husband is going to divorce you." To which she reacted like Mariyah had said a bad word in a conference! She jerked backwards and looked at Mariyah accusingly. Mind you, she is the one who had been saying this for almost a year. Now Mariyah says it and Mariyah becomes the bad one! Then Mariyah added,

"In fact, he has already divorced you." Pause. She gasped audibly. "*Imagine* you are divorced. How is life without a husband, girl? Not so bad right? What is the worst that can happen" She started crying, yet, just as quickly, she started smiling while the initial tears had not yet rolled off her eyes.

The rest of the day in the office she was her old self that was loved so much. She was the funny, rambunctious, lady-tomboy her husband had fallen in love with more than twenty-five years earlier.

The next day, she brought Mariyah a yellow candle as a thank you gift. They are still very happily married.

When you mentally live what you are so afraid of it, it runs away. You also realize it is not so bad after all and it might even be sweeter or a doorway to the great unknown! Unblock your blocks.

All is color coded within. In my teens I learned this sentence that I have since used, "our personal dispositions are like window panes through which we see the world either as rosy or dull. What we see is at times actually colored from the inside rather than from the outside." Change the inside and the color code outside would change.

Antidote to Fear. Fear brings much unhappiness. "Be strong and courageous. Do not be afraid or terrified because of them, for the Lord your God goes with you; he will never leave you nor forsake you." To me, fear is not "false evidence appearing real" as many suggest. Whoever says that is probably sitting in a plush house or office and driving on tarred roads. They have not experienced the following fears manifesting:

91

They have not walked barefooted on roads with sharp stones that with every step you take the pain goes straight to your heart. The resulting pain is real, nothing false about it. Neither have they experienced the daily ('fear of') headaches and dizziness brought by going for days or weeks without food; they have not been afraid of being sold, raped, or molested repeatedly; they have never seen other kids going to school while they had no one to sponsor them; they have never been left with ten kids to feed by a husband overseas or in the city and the kids are crying of real hunger and illness and no shoes or books; they have never been whopped by those in control; they have never lived in anticipation of the night where for sure they will be prostituted by their mother while she watches; neither have they seen limbs – arms, fingers, legs cut off daily by gem hunters and you or another are next. This is real! Nothing false about it!

No need to debate what fear is to different people; the key is to be strong and courageous and to believe as discussed in another section above in a deity bigger and stronger than you. Then, go through which is the formula, the law of nature, like birthing. Just like the blade of grass cracking through the pavement, go through and nature will protect you and take care of the rest. Do not wonder how, that is nature's job, it knows how. The energy of 'going through' with courage sometimes destroys the 'pleasure' energy of the evil doer and they give up or slack just enough for you to slip through.

Detach. Learn to let it go! Learn how to detach… If you do not hit the "send" button, your email stays in draft mode… for years. You can edit all you want; it can only be effective if released. Hit "send" and forget about it. The same technique applies when you resolve issues and give to a higher power to solve. Let it go, so the "routers" can deliver to them so whoever is responsible can work on your demand. Detachment is very powerful and a key to success and happiness. Learn how to, if you can't do it on your own, hire a coach to aid in you mastering it. Even when you 'believe', without detachment, manifestation will not happen.

Excerpt from Love Under the Kola Nut Tree. What City Moms Didn't Tell You About Creating Fulfilling Relationships:

"Praying, then dwelling, and mulling on the problem does not release it. It is like saving an email in draft format only to edit it and re-edit it. It will never serve its purpose until you release it so the routers can route it to the right destination. Man-made systems are the microcosm of spiritual or macro systems. As above, so below.

Sawdust

Though we might not intend to, all our actions have side effects. The carpenter in making your beautiful curio or bed produces sawdust. When you cook, you create trash from the peelings. There are human by-products. When you come together with a partner, you generate heat and more.

Basically from when God created the world or if we choose the big bang theory, there were by-products. A lot of the things on earth then are stardust from the "big bang" or from the "Word." It is in and from this dust or by-product that most evil, toxins, and bacteria evolve. We need to be conscious of it.

In relationships, all our actions create by-products that can build or destroy our relationships. Being mindful of these phenomena is akin to getting into the gab spiritually. This begins to happen when we practice *detachment*. *'Let it go'*, as we say, is a very powerful spiritual technique. As you begin to observe without being judgmental you begin to see the dust particles and you develop the wisdom to manage them. You cannot destroy matter, but you can convert it into a more beneficial form.

Learn Non-resistance (in different situations), especially in relationships. It will guarantee joy. Here is an example of how Rose handled this regarding relationships.

"If Rose did not like or love a man, there was nothing in this whole wide earth he could do to make her like or love him period. Know thyself. Neither can you make anybody romantically love you no matter how much you cajole them or shower them with material possessions. In cases of real desperate men, Rose pretended to be back with them until they calmed down and then she vamoosed. That is when she developed the polite technique or the rule of nonresistance.

"Evil energy needs something to feed on just like a hungry person needs food," she explained to me, as we sat eating mangoes and licking the delicious juice off our fingers.

"Evil energy needs evil energy as its food, but when you refuse to fight back it is at a loss of what to do. So the evil energy gradually dissipates as it starves to death."

If you hit a tree, because the tree resists, you might break it or break your body parts or car. If you hit a corn plant that just bends with the flow of things, neither the plant nor you get badly hurt.

This technique of nonresistance can be used in so many ways to diffuse potentially explosive situations. The only way we succeed is to *rise above the situation*. But this calls for *self-mastership*, as the flesh likes revenge and a hurting heart can conjure devious punishments.

Rising above a situation in most cases implies you have to learn to let go; you have to know who you are and not fight losing battles. Nobody can disrespect you if you know who you are. They can say things or portray behavior or body language that evokes disrespect. You can choose to flow into their negative energy and experience what they are trying hard to inflict on you or you can simply choose to say, "That is not me. I know who I am and I am not going to

94

stoop to your level".

People only fight at a level where they have a chance to win. In elementary school a crippled classmate of mine could beat up the big boys in class and in the school. This was because once a fight started he tackled his opponent in such a way he brought them to their knees, eye to eye with him. Then he beat the crap out of them. Once the center of gravity they were used to changed they lost control of their bearings and he was in his element. They had not learned to fight while on their knees or their buttocks. While his legs were lanky and weak his upper body was built up powerfully. Know yourself; know thy strengths and weaknesses.

If you do not know who you are and do not have a personal constitution, ethical values, or know the kind of things you would or would not do, say or not say, you will be easily shepherded into other people's zone of operation. - An excerpt from Love Under the Kola Nut Tree, What City Moms Didn't Tell You About Creating Fulfilling Relationships.

Forgive. All of these points above will be hard to make you happy if you do not forgive and if you are not truthful with yourself. If you cannot forgive, stop looking for solutions, as permanent manifestation is not going to happen and stick permanently. Wait to proceed with your search for anything, until you decide to forgive first. Do not even waste your time or that of praying people or groups. Forgiveness is so important on the journey to whatever that the Lord Himself tells us, so by putting it in the Lord's Prayer (Hint...) it is a pre-requisite for your success! In the dialect, forgiveness translates into either "a loan," or "something you found." Tomorrow is another day.

Consider this: the body holds emotions and energy in certain organs. Example, we know about the heart and love, the stomach and stress, the liver and anger. In the village, sometimes when healing is not happening for someone, they are asked to search their mind and forgive. The reason is because when we do not forgive, we block healing to our own selves. The unfortunate thing is that the physical body has cycles as in disease cycles. So let's say, you had an illness that if, say, blood does not flow to that organ after a certain period, the organ degenerates irretrievably. You lie in the hospital being pumped with drugs but you are not healing; and the best doctors are getting confused and edging towards doubt of their skills and why their medicine is not working. You on the other hand hold the key... anger and un-forgiveness. You not being able to forgive, blocks the flow of healing energy – thus to the sick organ also.

If by some chance you come to your senses being coaxed by a family member, friend, or priest to forgive and let go, you do finally forgive. Unfortunately, the sick body part's disease cycle can't wait for your emotions so it degenerates and dies. By the time you forgive it is too late to save the organ and if it is a life-sustaining organ that dies, you die also! Any doubt why the Lord, Jesus Himself, put this (forgiveness) in the only thing (prayer) that the disciples asked to be taught? They knew He had another trick within His prayers because His were more effective than theirs so they wanted it! Even, He asked people if they wanted to be healed before he healed them, else they would have blocked their own healing.

Forgive. It can be hard, I agree; so the other secret is to love your neighbor as you love YOU. If you love YOU, then you will want the best for you. So love your neighbor by forgiving them... to get back to you. Forgiveness thus, opens much to YOU. (Always comes back to self doesn't it? ahhhh!) If you want permanent

96

manifestation, take the forgiveness pill and move on to another level in this journey!

Ride under someone else's shadow of success, strength, and network. Get a piggyback ride on someone successful to your destination. (Also see topic below: **Selling After the Market Has Closed**) Don't be gung-ho about doing or getting it done "all by yourself." It will take you a longer time and lots of frustration and unhappiness. And by the time you get there, it might be obsolete. Thus...

Use a Mastermind group - (short cuts). Do not struggle to solve a problem that someone already has a solution for. ("Where two or three are gathered in my name, I am there with them," Jesus says in the Bible.) Then in another section He says, "Again I say to you, that if two of you agree on earth about anything that they may ask, it shall be done for them by My Father who is in heaven."

Even Jesus had a "mastermind group" of various levels (I call it that to understand better). Even when God wanted to create Man or destroy man's dubious plans He said "Let Us..." go do this thing together. There is power in "numbers"! If God "masterminds"...hint, hint, do it; God loves numbers, and multiplication... big brother to addition! Get some help; discipline your ego and ask for help. If you cannot form one, pay to join one – a quality mastermind group. Ask for proof of success of the members as you search for the right one for you. Check my website and join one of my mastermind groups - http://estherlamnyam.com/coaching/mastermind-groups.

(Hint, hint, you do not have to be a Christian for the laws quoted above to work for you! These rules do not have religious restrictions, creed, color attached to them. Now we see why some people of non-descript religions are highly successful!)

Ask and it will be given to you! Many people get unhappy because someone failed to give to them. Sometimes people do not know we wanted "something." Best bet is to kick your ego to the side and ask. The worst that can happen is the person says "no", "not now", "later", or just a seed has been planted. Most times we get a "yes." Consider the guy who wants to marry a girl whom he already knows wants to marry him. If he does not ask, it will not happen. Laws are laws.

If you are a Bible reader, you will notice that Jesus said in John 16:24: "Until now you have *asked nothing* in my name. **Ask**, and **you** will **receive**, that **your** joy may be **full**." Pre-requisite is asking, second is receiving. They have to go together! Are you asking? Are you receiving? Do you know how to receive?

Some of us have been so used all of our lives to giving that when someone gives us anything, even a hug, we become very uncomfortable and do not know how to receive. The joy we got when giving, we take away from someone else when we fail to receive.

Homework: Learn to receive. Be Receptive. When someone gives you anything, say, "thank you." Smile and do not say something like, "oh, it's nothing" yah, you will wiggle a bit because it feels uncomfortable but hang in tight; allow the other person to feel the joy of your receiving.

Do not start telling stories about how you do not really need this, "oh it is okay", "don't worry about it", "I can do it all by myself", etc., so on and so forth. For most of us, this is a continuous learning skill, but to the African villager, they have mastered the art of receiving!

98

A big lesson I learned about giving and receiving:

Africans give and receive hugs because in our culture it is just a natural thing to do …share energy. But I got a bigger lesson in giving and receiving hugs when I traveled to another state many years ago and visited a friend I had not seen in years.

I had communicated with his girlfriend, but had not met her until then. Upon hearing our excited voices, she came out of the room where she had been taking a nap. We were both very excited to see each other and in traditional African fashion we hugged. She, I believe, might not have registered this experience the way I did, as she had a more village presence while I was brought up away from the village. The village will teach you no matter where you are, if you are receptive!

After we hugged, instead of pulling away, she just stood there dropping her arms, while I had my arms around her. But she would not pull away. At that moment, everything stood still for me, and I received someone giving themselves to me (energy of love, peace, friendship, welcome home, I missed you, I finally get to see you, be in your presence and you in mine, you need this hug, I need to be embraced). Hundreds of peaceful, loving, gentle, kind energies floated into my being. I received her gift, almost twenty years later I still remember; better yet I have used it to harmonize others. At the time I received it, I did not know I would be doing this work today. To give you have to receive. When you receive you give. Ask to be able to receive. Ask to be able to give. It is a law of nature, ask and it shall be given to you. Nature does not lie you know, it always keeps its word. Sometimes, just sit quietly and listen; listen to voice or no voice!

What is the pre-requisite to receive?

_____.

Travaux Pratiques:

1. Give a hug as described above.
2. Journal the experience.
3. Repeat often.
4. Heal yourself and others.

Selling after the market has closed. Don't sell after the market has closed. Work with rhythms.

Work in sync with nature. Show up when you are supposed to. Do your homework always. Explanation in this blog I wrote:

Selling After the Market has Closed

> I used to hear this saying: "You are selling after the market has closed", when in boarding school in my middle school years.

> When students showed up after events, meetings, and concerts had finished and then tried to participate or give their point of view, other students told them they were trying to sell after the market had closed. Basically, they were late and it was time to move on to the next item on the schedule or they had already moved on. They had to live with the consequences!

> We all have heard the saying: "there is a time and season for everything" under the sun. When we understand the cycles and rhythms of nature, life, relationships, and businesses, we stop fighting against the tide and start sailing with the wind to

100

create great success.

There are certain things that can only be accomplished at certain times of the year, month, day, and hour. The ninth hour's energy is very different from the fifth hour. Women have their periods (or cycle) at certain times in a twenty-eight day cycle. Men have cycles too, which most of them choose not to acknowledge and tap into. Corn grows for a certain number of days; gestation of babies is a certain number of months. Every illness has its natural life cycle and an incubation period. You cannot burst an abscess or zit before it is ready.

There is summer, fall, spring, and winter, which businesses tap into that to plan for inventory and sales.

Understand the cycles and phases of nature. The trick is to know when to tap into this life cycle and then harness or harvest during the period of peak performance and productivity, because this oscillation will soon change phase. For example, we know when to tap into a woman's cycle and have a baby. You can try all you want at "off peak" times and you would only come out empty.

Learn the cycles of the things and people in your life, job, and relationship and tap into that. In the village, traders knew when to hoard produce and store for the time when the seasons would change and there would be no more produce. Then they sold all they had hoarded at exorbitant prices.

If you were in tune with the cycle and rhythm of your life and nature, the rain, snow, sun, or moon's traffic would not bother you. Instead you will learn to work with them to achieve your results. Thieves know this; they come out mostly in the night or when you are at work.

When we work with the cycles and rhythms of nature we are

101

bound to create balance and harmony in all we do. However, the first pre-requisite to achieving this is to know yourself (which I will cover in other blogs). This knowledge will enable you not to sell after the market has closed.

One of the reasons geese fly in V formation is because it enables them to conserve their energy. This is because of the reduction of wind resistance created by each bird flying slightly above the bird in front of him. They are working with the laws of nature! It becomes effortless and they can fly for a very long time before stopping for rest (another cycle!).

Take a moment and examine your life and relationships in regards to some constant issues you keep having. Are you selling after the market has closed? When we work off-rhythm we are bound to get frustrated, stressed, and hence invite disease into our bodies. Most illnesses result from working against the 'wind' and trying to brute, force it. Save yourself some headache and work with the laws of nature and see how things become effortless.

Be still and know you. Imitate nature and create a fulfilling life.

 (From http://estherlamnyam.com/selling-after-the-market-has-closed)

Pay for what you receive. Ground to manifest. Pay somehow; pay it forward. This will make you really happy giving again! (Repeated tip.)

An electrician would not dare work without being sure of grounding. Energy (via word, physical, material things, or thoughts) needs to be grounded. Whatever we receive is a form of energy. When not properly grounded, it eventually evaporates or dissipates. If you are working on things and repeatedly they are successful, and then fail, check your giving. If you cannot pay directly the giver, go give to a homeless person, a church, a mother, coworker, etc. When someone's ideas, especially someone you have not hired, benefit you tremendously, pay for it somehow. All energy moves and gets transmuted. If not grounded in giving or in food or dance, it dissipates and your business or marriage or relations snaps back to naught... years later... sob, sob, and sob. Some people's energy is so strong and pure that an idea from them can serve you for years. Remember cycles.... seasons eventually change. Laws of motion will become evident; and since the force or energy is no longer there to exert its influence on the concept, idea or whatever you "took" without paying, its acceleration will slowly and naturally slow down and come to rest! Oh, oh! Ever wonder why some people's success in businesses or relationships slowly "died" irretrievably?

(Similar to a point in "**Pay the Universe; also called Satikak or Sarakak in the village,**" above. For some reason, this point begs to be repeated in another way!). When you get success, a blessing, or avoid a bad thing do a Sarakak.

Do not steal. Especially, do not steal consciously knowing you are doing so. Confusing? Yeah, when this principle came to me, I had to also put my ear to the ground to get it!

Simple example, have you ever hung out with someone, invited someone to lunch, dinner, a function, called someone, or visited someone... secretly knowing that what you really wanted to do is "pick their brains" for their sense that they worked so hard for but without directly telling them so? Ah ha! (The Spirit knows the real desires of your heart; the truth! No matter what you tell yourself.)

"What is wrong with this?" you may ask. So long as you are clear and you honor them for what they have offered without a secret agenda it is okay. I believe we should share our gifts. If people feel bad or used when they later discover what your real plan was, even years later, therein lies my point. Sometimes, inadvertently, their angry energy destroys your projects and happiness. (Meet Toni and all his furious ex-girlfriends and baby mamas in Love Under the Kola Nut Tree) Seriously, this is not a laughing matter. To be happy, try not to (consciously) engineer your own demise.

Have you told someone an idea; soon thereafter they implemented it as their own? I believe the commandment is really not "Thou shalt not steal" but "Thou *cannot* steal". Thou should not steal is easier to understand. Case in point, those who steal keep stealing... because the spiritual well of wealth never belonged to them so they are never satisfied or it does not hit the spot so to speak. We all make mistakes, but much unhappiness comes later when nature corrects errors and spiritual principles always override even many, many years later. Whatever is done in darkness eventually comes to light. The villagers say, "Truth is slow, but it always arrives."

Do not architect your sadness by stealing. Honor people by telling them you need their intelligence instead of stealing in the guise of lunch or whatever; even when you pay for lunch, your intention was to steal. Their idea they gave you might be worth millions or thousands of dollars. If you want to convince yourself that the $10.00 or $100.00 lunch is what they deserved, that is your choice. Pay for what you receive...tip. Cover your butt!

Cycles. Understand cycles as discussed in this text. Understand correspondence and reflex points in your affairs. Which buttons do you push to get certain results from others? Careful observation will let you know the formulas you and others use. If unhappy with the outcomes, maybe we are using formulas that do not benefit all.

 Have no grey areas. Always be clear about your stance, focus, direction, etc. Sometimes we are unhappy because we confuse others by always changing our position. If we are an authority figure people might not have the courage to correct us. They end up leaving the corporation or relationships and one or both parties may be unhappy about this.

Use colors of the rainbow to harmonize your day, week, and life.
Colors bring different energies into our lives. Just changing the color of a piece of clothing will leave you feeling much excitement and joy. **Color-code your day.** Each day, each season has a color. This affects us tremendously whether we are aware of it or not.

Example: Years ago, I was attending a week-long seminar. By the weekend, an elderly lady came to me and said, "dearie, stop wearing all those dark colors. They are not good for you." I had never heard anything about colors, but I believed her. My wardrobe was full of black and white. It took me more than four years to brighten my wardrobe completely. Benefits: I feel much more energized when I dress up; my mind is clear and excited ("for no obvious reason"), I get plenty of happy feedback and when I look at myself sometimes in the mirror when I dress up colorfully in the morning and go "whistle, whistle". (Hmmm, guess I forgot my African roots... seen their colorful garb?)

Use colors around the house and in bedrooms, you will reap the benefits. God was not doodling when he put the colors of the season. Just imagine the colors of Fall, the blue sky, the green in

105

the leaves and trees, etc. Even the seasons change color; imitate nature to be happy.

Homework: Find out more about color and use more color in your life and graph your happiness daily.

Do not pretend to be present in relationships! Be present; give your presence. Do not waste other people's time. It makes both you and them unhappy, as the spirit knows the truth all the time.

Let me use a car example to clarify this point: Years ago I bought a used car that started having issues the very next day! Three years later I still had the car. The trouble now was that if while the car was running I stopped at say a stop sign, the car would cut off... aahh yah yah! Living paycheck to paycheck with repeated car repairs was a nightmare. Worst of all, no mechanic could figure out what the issue was.

I used to work at a car repair shop and when it closed, most of the mechanics started their own shops. One very young man called Xandra was a car repair genius. He now had his own shop to which I took my car. His workers put my truck on the lift, ran tests like all the other shops I had gone to, yet they found nothing that was causing the car to cut off when I stopped at a stop sign or light and not start back. I became an AAA (American Automobile Association) member after too many towing experiences and stress!

I knew in my heart if anyone could figure what was wrong with this car, it was Xandra. So I called him again and he told me his mechanics found nothing wrong with my car. So I implored him to check it out himself, just one more time. He obliged me... thankfully so we now can learn a BIG relationship lesson.

I believe he found out it was the starter. Now here is our lesson, the starter gave enough charge for circuit testers and other tools to detect a charge and eliminate it as the cause of the car stopping and not restarting. So it was not replaced and my woes continued. However, its connection (to the battery) was not strong enough to sustain the car when stopped.

Much unhappiness in relationships is wrought by people who are in our lives and seem alive on the front end to the world, but are not giving enough charge within the relationship to sustain it! Chew on this! It is a very sad and painful situation that is difficult to detect because they touch you like a cat, soft enough to make you feel their presence but that is the end of it. Killing you softly!

Be hot, or be cold, but again, stay away from grey areas... even the rainbow stays away from grey! Imitate nature.

Do not sit with your back to the door, especially if you are the leader of an organization. This creates a very defenseless atmosphere. This can bring you serious unhappiness!

Lesson by example: Years ago when I was still middle aged, I worked in a very successful company. In my second week I was sent to the owner's office to work on his computer. As I walked into the huge office with huge plants, I noticed his back was completely to the door. I got a very uncomfortable feeling. I knew he should not be sitting like that but I was new, young, and inexperienced. The following week I felt very convicted to have knowledge that could help him but did not tell him. At the same time I was kind of a peon! I prayed about it and I knew I should tell him about this situation. Then I prayed for courage to rise up in me. Finally a few weeks later, I was sent to his office again. After finishing solving the computer issue that sent me there, I gathered courage prayerfully and said to him,

"Sir, may I say something not computer related to you?"

"Sure" he replied.

"Well…. Well… what I have to say… if you do not like it, please do not throw me away, throw but the thing I say away,"

"Okay," he smiled, "what is it?"

(Courage, hang with me …breath in deep and out)

"The way you are sitting is not good. Do not sit with your back to the door." I said gingerly.

"Really? Okay. Thank you" he replied.

I left his office; shaking in the aftermath… did I just say that to the CEO, Owner, and Founder of a thirty-year-old global cooperation?

Every week I passed by his office, I observed he was still sitting with his back to the door. About three months later, I asked him,

"Did you think about what I told you?"

To which he replied, "I told my wife what you said and she said she understood what you meant." So he had listened to me and remembered! Hm! But guess what? This man never changed his desk arrangement, to sit facing the door or with the door to his right or left.

One day two years later, we were all invited to a big all-company function in another part of the county. The vice president stood up with his hands proudly on his hips and announced.

"I am now the new CEO of this company. This is the happiest day of my life!" He paused, looking around gloatingly.

"I replace Mr. X, (the owner and founder) who will stay in position Y until he does not have majority ownership."

You could have heard a pin drop before the applause, which I believe mostly was mechanical. They kept the owner only as long as it took them to buy back shares he owned. Off course I could not eat any of the goodies provided that evening ...many of us did not. Hush, hush talk happened the next few weeks at work by very sad faces!

Ousted so easily! A man in his late sixties, losing the thing his passion had built at a time when he should have been reaping the joy of how he had changed lives positively. There is no way for me to tell if had he not been sitting in such an inauspicious position he would have continued on as the owner, but I believe it would not have hurt him to try. You can learn a lot even from a donkey... if you are receptive!

As we have been observing in this book, the joy stealers are sometimes the intangibles!

Do not build solid walls around your houses, use fences or rods. When I travel internationally to some African countries, the bricks and stone-walls around many houses are amazing. Sometimes I drive around just to admire them or take pictures.

When you fence yourself in, you not only block thieves and beggars or whatever else you want to block, you block good luck, good health, good fortune, and more. The good and the bad are blocked. If you observe carefully, the supposedly rich who live in those "fortresses", just go round and round in cycles. How does it

109

profit them to drink champagne, wine, and eat big meals daily when the neighbor on the other side of the wall lives in a hut? Life is not joyous when you observe most of these people. Always scheming, using offshore accounts. Sleeping with one eye open!

Energy flows in to those compounds but cannot flow out and does not. They dwell in dead stagnant energy, hence the continuing in stagnating behaviors. Dying of sophisticated illnesses. Beware! Laws of nature do not give a hoot about our plunders or grandiosities. Any wonder why America and Europe without solid opaque walls around houses are doing great while these African countries, rich as they are, only day dream of such greatness? The villagers might live in the open, but the leaders through whom energy is programmed by nature and through inaugurations and coronations to flow to the populace, live in stagnant energy. The currency does not flow …is not current (or only 'flows' to their accounts abroad). When they die, the children they have trained continue with this tomfoolery. Imitate nature!

Learn the basics thoroughly before moving on. Get the technique, arithmetic, or physics correct before becoming creative. This will ensure you do not waste your time and get things that can be done in two months done in two years or cost lives! This brings a lot of frustrations and unhappiness, and some finally just give up because of repeated failure. I know there is a mentality of "fire, then aim". If you study those teaching this, they "aimed" first; meaning they took the time to learn the basics. Shorts cuts are good when you know the principles behind the tool so you can error correct on the fly in case of an emergency. Know the scenarios to use this; else disasters and unhappiness and even death are close by!

Understand verbal contracts and the power of the spoken word and thoughts. Wireless communication existed long before there was wireless communication, as we know it today via technology. All your thoughts and words are creative. To be happy, think thoughts that yield the end results you want. Many people become unhappy because of the imaginings in their hearts and minds and with words of their lips. Think and speak light into your being. Thus manage your thoughts. This point alone will change your whole life, business, health, and lead to happiness.

Mind the guy called O'clock to be happy. O'clock is a guy I met at birth. He is always with me and moves on whether I am ready or not. I need him. He is life. Many of us have a distorted view of time or O'clock (By now you must have figured out I probably need this little book more than you do ☺).

A lot of unhappiness comes when we do not plan well, or something comes up as it always would and we end up stressed because the time is off. Time will not change because we woke up late or there is traffic as discussed somewhere in this text. Learn from O'clock and imitate his ways. Even if you end up a few minutes late, your stress levels will be low and your happiness quotient high.

Renew your knowledge, renew yours goals, and renew your mind often. Renew. Things change! Plug into a power and human beings that will help you renew your aspirations, mindsets, and processes to a direction of success. Be mindful of your acquaintances, as they will rub off on you and you on them.

The people we hang around with will uplift our energy, flatten it or down it. We take on the atmosphere created and soon seamlessly become that which we do not like by unconsciously becoming that very vice. If one day you wake up and query yourself why you now gossip, complain about your elders/leaders, or family members so much more. Pull back and observe your life and interactions with those in it. You will notice the genesis of this behavior. Sometimes it starts with us just listening and not even chiming in, months or years later we have adapted and it becomes the obvious conversations with certain folks.

Another way to easily observe this point is to note discussions when in different countries, groups, and with different friends and family. **Mind the atmosphere created by two or more**. You can see why when people who do not give often come to the U.S., they start giving more after a while and may even become more patriotic; then, they move back to their country and snap right back ...ehm ehm...

Ask for a personal performance review from friends, coworkers, and family ...hang in tight and stomach it like a (woman) man. It is bitter medicine that will move the needle of your growth by leaps! But you have to be strong to hear what others think about behavior that is not becoming.

I discovered this by 'error.' I gave genuine unsolicited feedback to a very good friend in the nineties about a certain behavioral trait they manifested in public and in meetings that put them contrary to others. It was done in good faith, as I grew up in boarding school and in a family that corrected our errors promptly. Two weeks later, he sat me down and listed behaviors I had that he also thought were contrary. It was painful to take, but I did not try to explain the behavior or his points off but honored him and my earlier review of him by being quiet. At times, I felt like crawling under the table and hiding, but I sat there while my stomach churned and took it! Then, I thanked him! (*Now get out of my apartment!*)

From that experience, I have over and over solicited this personal review from friends, coworkers, kids, etc. Most of the time we do not know we do certain things that make us come across in "unhealthy" ways. However, when pointed out, every time we raise our hand to do it again, the observation peeps out and reminds us to fix it, and if we care to improve as individuals on legitimate observations, we work on it. It could be as simple as making a gesture with a finger that in Africa is okay but in America might get you beat up only if lucky! This is not a performance review at work (though that helps too) for corporate work and pay issues.

We might be upset and complain about someone for a behavior they do not even know they do. Think about it this way, any sane person will not be consciously doing something many people or coworkers complain about if they knew it.

As we purify, improve, refine, and renew, we get better and manifest our desires faster with more fun thus yielding greater happiness.

DO NOT marry under a religious leader or authority if you do not understand spiritual relationships, spiritual rules, and deities. Yes, you heard me right! Ever since I could think, I have always asked questions and

113

troubleshooting is one of my fortes in the information technology world where I currently make my living.

In coaching and dealing with people in the West who have failed marriages, while there are some main similarities, most marriages under religious authority = limited life span of marriages. (I have no stats just village goggles.) Have you ever wondered why people live for years happily and even having tons of kids, and then one day some religious authority pronounces them husband and wife and blesses them using a religious book and soon thereafter divorce proceedings are in the works?

So I started looking into this and among many reasons, the main one is that we are spiritual beings in a physical body. There are spiritual forces that are around us and respond to our actions, thoughts, and words at all times. (Non-spiritual forces too: If I leave a cut melon in the trashcan, maggots show up – effortlessly!)

When we consciously invite spiritual deities into our lives and do not pay attention to what that means from the deities' point of view, problems are bound to ensue whether we like it or not. Some of the ceremonies we invite deities into are marriages, coronations, and inaugurations of presidents and political leaders. Do not invite deities and ignore them; they don't play that game! I do not think they directly cause your relationship to fail; the spiritual principles being violated engineer the failure. It is like a physics or mathematical equation, or the If, Then, Else flowchart as in computer programming. We unknowingly invite failure to our relationships by bringing in spiritual forces that do not take a background position and then ignoring them!

These activities that involve spiritual realms are not for show. Growing up, I did not know this (oh well, maybe just so I

114

can now believe and help others!), and wondered why we did these ceremonies and did not believe those words mattered but just some text to say. But there is an experience I had that keeps coming to my mind as I write this tip that begs me to tell you. I will write it and hopefully I will not chicken out and delete it before publication. If you see just the title "My president reprimand", without the story, know I chickened out.

Lesson by example: **My president reprimand:** Two years before President George W. Bush left office, I returned home from work one evening and stood in front of my television listening to him talk. I can't remember his topic because I was not interested in hearing it, as I was mentally "complaining" or "murmuring" about the ongoing war and how it was wrong and how he xyz. How mothers were losing their sons and daughters because of a war initiated on false information. I honestly cannot remember the mental dialog I was having with *myself but I know* it was not nice!

Then I heard the LORD drop it into my ear, loud and clearly, "Watch your mouth, (and called my name ☹!). You voted for him. You got me involved in this; now watch what you say about him."

Do I need to tell you I ran away from my family room and television? A good preacher can preach ten sermons from this sentence!

In the spiritual, whether I voted for him in the physical does not matter anymore, as once we put leaders in office, we all by default voted for him/them – corporately! Say I, I. Yes you did! ☺ And welcome to the club! Once we appoint leaders, we are not supposed to destroy them mentally, verbally, scripturally, etc.

...ESPECIALLY if we invited God - a deity into it! I may have heard this along the way, but it did not register into my consciousness the impact of what that meant. However, spiritual and natural laws like gravity work whether we know them or not!

Are we supposed to not 'criticize' leaders? Up for debate probably. Not destructively in my case! However, I now try having constructive criticism or shut up! Yes, me! We can debate, trouble shoot, brain storm, etc.; but not curse, speak against, and destroy leaders, especially those whom WE have asked to put their hand on a spiritual book, the Bible in the case of our presidents and leaders; and then we have invited that spiritual Being... collectively into the president's leadership over us. If you want to do it, you do it; but me, hmm, I am not inviting "leprosy" into my life ...consciously oh.

Some of us do not have the liberty to be flippant. Grow and learn, learn and grow; certain gifts and responsibilities come with big time restrictions and regulations.

Point here is that, we should be mindful of the vows we take and the spirits we invite into our affairs... that show up in earnest! Do we? This is not for show as I've found out!

Still want to marry in church? Hehehe! Get to know the deity and his or her rules first and mind that deity's presence throughout the relationship or what you invited them into. These are some of the foxes that bring unhappiness!

Develop a habit of journaling and carrying a notebook with you. Many poems, ideas, and books can be downloaded to paper or digital devices when they float into your mind and saved for later. How can this make you happy?

- If you worry or have too much mental dialog going on inside your head, downloading on paper has a way of clearing our mind. (Remember, thoughts are concrete things.)
- You can write a whole book this way.
- Some brilliant ideas are so crystal clear at the moment you get them that if you do not write the words verbatim at that time, later you may forget and become unhappy. In fact my book "Love Under the Kola Nut Tree. What City Moms Didn't Tell You About Creating Fulfilling Relationships" was mostly written in the morning on the train (Metro) on my way to work. Great ideas will float into my mind, so clearly and powerfully, that I would pull my notebook and pen, write a few paragraphs and expand on them at night when home or on the weekends. If I did not write them at the time, try as hard as I could, I would not remember them, nor the word choice and flow and arrangement of the words.
- Create your own knowledge base (million dollar idea …yes …glad you remember…I take tips …Sarakak at www.estherlamnyam.com). I developed this idea by accident many years ago in the nineties when personal digital assistants (PDA) were the thing. Then one day the battery died and I lost all my contacts (not like

today when there are back up options and the Cloud). I started a knowledge base to keep phone numbers and tidbits. You can take hours to solve a problem; years or weeks later, if the problem arises most of us will not remember. Even with Google search, there are still ideas, passwords, where you met contacts, recipes, menus, how your crafted something or solved a problem or a health problem that only you know. Might look minor then, but it later comes in handy and will bring a smile of relief to your face or a pat by you on your own back! You can write a whole book or blog out of one point that floated into your mind during someone's speech, sermon, or a word you heard in a dream ...if you can remember it!

Hmmm... even some things I am sharing with you in this happiness book came from such an effort! Whoa! While the standard guru texts are effective, these homemade one of a kind recipes, I am sharing with you, will also move the dial for you faster and permanently. Hurrah!

Honor Relationships. Honor each other. Helps us fight with love.

*Understand intersections. What I refer to as "Inevitable Intersections," happen every time two or more people, ideas, countries, etc. come together for any purpose. To live harmoniously with others and be happy you have to understand intersections. Every entity involved is going to bring notions, some spot on; some perceived mindsets; cultural indoctrinations, religious indoctrinations, and more. Take time to understand the

118

whole picture and the different visions. Then see where they intersect based on the goal you are currently working on. With this understanding, you can solve issues, and also postulate ideas that will work to the benefit of all involved. (Draw two or three overlapping circles. The middle area where all circles are included, is an example of an intersection in mathematics. This applies to relationships and businesses as well.)

Keep coming back to this intersection, as here, everyone that is involves' vision is being catered to. This point can make you millions; it can save you millions, help you create worthwhile relationships, and even prolong your life. (Yes, this is a tip (Sarakak ☺) point.)

The biggest intersection is, as above, so below; as below, so above. Work in the intersection in these two opposite facing concepts or triangles if you draw them. Mind the intersection in the middle!

We are spiritual beings in a physical cocoon; know and integrate the spirit side in all you do. Happiness can be yours if you do so.

Learn the pre-requisites. Much unhappiness is wrought by hurrying. Lay a good foundation first. Without doing the groundwork, it makes it easier to fail when we move on to advanced concepts and another phase of relationships.

Learn a new language. Modulate your intonations! This might sound strange on your way to happiness land. Let me attempt to explain. 'Attempt' only, because, any verbal or written language is a limitation to our communication. Word play, word positioning, and misunderstanding due to language differences have engineered a lot of misunderstandings of each other and relationship failures. Learn a new language and translate words or sentences and try to understand from a different perspective. Nonverbal body language and gesticulations speak volumes.

A marriage broke up because the man called the woman a word that meant something really bad in her culture. He did not mean (much) harm but it was in the hit of a marital argument. They were both from different continents.

In another situation that eventually ended in divorce, the woman complained that when she called her husband's name he responded very harshly, "What?" This startled her every time, dissociated her energy and chemistry, and being lovey-dovey took a while to happen. His dialect of origin is powerful so it was difficult for him to see her point.

As explained in my blog post that lead to this book, sound is quite powerful. Do not sing derogatory songs hoping your mate will get the message. They will, but they will also see your evil side, and shelf that for a fighting day! Use your language, songs, vowel sounds, body language properly if you want to be happy and have a happy home and relationships.

French men are alleged to be the most romantic, though also rumored as arrogant and egotistical as you can have (yes, perceptions and reality). Looking into why they are dubbed to be romantic, some of it is mostly the way they intone their words, the softness of word undulations/pronunciation, play with words, sound/resonance, calm feel of the word delivery, smile in their voice, and perceived 'presence' in such a way you can feel it even if not looking at them or over the phone.

Until when I discovered the power in a name, I was not too conscious of my name; however, my French buddies, (looking

120

back) kept it alive for me until then. One in particular when he called my name… it was always like a question mark, a journey, gentle waves on a pristine beach, forget all worries …you name it. This, always, I noted, made me smile inside no matter what. (Note: when people are in wooing mode, they tune into their connecting self… but that aside, you get the point here.)

Name-calling (or without reverence) has been known to start fights.

One more point about language: remember that language is very limiting and it is practically impossible for us to put into words the vastness in our heart and minds. Thus be mindful of this limitation in relationships and don't get bent out of shape when others can't express "properly" (in the way, behavior or language you wanted). Remember that different languages were created to divide and not to unite!

Not lost in translation. One more point on language☺! When you translate into another language, it will help you understand the situation more and show you how to solve issues. For example though we already discussed forgiveness, let me use that example here. So, I take the word forgive and say it in my dialect as "forshih meh" meaning "forgive me." As I start breaking the word further and further down, I notice it translates to many concepts, which are:

- Give me a loan (of…)
- Forgive me
- For - give me.
- Loan me (…)

- Find or discover me, pick me up from the ground (as when you find unexpected money or something precious while taking a walk)
- My primordial compound has burned down

As you can see, forgiveness burns the old paradigm that does not work anymore; it discovers you and gives you a "loan" to use for whatever! (For buying time or peace or health or your heart's desire.) No doubt that the Lord put it in the Lord's Prayer among so many things He could have put in that prayer! Thus, do a little translation to be happy. Just because your partner used a certain word does not mean you should be broken...translate ...and you might find or discover you!

Your Travaux Pratiques or Homework: Eavesdrop! ...Ah ha! Listen to how lovers speak to each other. One very tough network administrator used to make me joyously smile though he was not talking to me but to his girlfriend on the phone. We shared an office and every time he spoke to his girlfriend, he was a completely different human being...not one who cursed at machines, network cables, and users with I. D. 10. T. issues!

Second Travaux Pratiques on language: Listen to YOU talk to others.

What/how does it make you feel?

_____

What elements do you want to enhance?

_____

What elements do you want to change?

_____

Will you follow through and change and enhance?
_____When? _____

Schedule a follow up on you by you! Date:

_____

Listen to folks whose relationships you admire. Learn, adapt, and upgrade. None of us were born with a relationship handbook. Read, study, and practice.

More about language – Invest in "understanding" and "comprehension" leading to wisdom to be happy: 'can' is not 'may'. Example, fill in the blanks:

Just because I can _____does not mean I may_____.

Just because I can _____does not mean I may_____.

Just because I can _____does not mean I may_____.

Just because I can _stay out late/smoke/curse/beat someone, etc. does not mean I may_ stay out late/smoke/curse/beat someone, etc.____.

Just because she/he said, "do not be foolish" does not mean she/he said, "I am foolish." It is just *advice, a head's up,* or an *observation* and not an insult (*comprehension!*) But if you know you are, then you choose to change you.

123

This little point has killed...dead...many relationships! That is why I overemphasize language/communication.

Invest in good nutrition, good food, and a good mattress. This is a well-known point, but we will point it out here because it begs to be. Feed your cells and they will help keep you happy. (Coming soon a book on "weight maintenance" as learned from the villagers. Visit my website often and get on my mailing list so you know when I develop new products – www.estherlamnyam.com)

Sneeze. Sneeze loud and strong! Yes you heard me right. Do not suffocate your sneezes. A lot of unhappiness and lethargy is brought by very low energy in us. Illness, bad company, bad news, parasites, low energy food, etc. can be the cause to lower our vibration to that which is good for stress, unhappiness, tiredness, low libido, disease, etc.

However, we can increase our physiology to a healthy state that produces endorphins and alertness by exercise. One of the quickest ways to raise your vibrational energy to levels that disease will run away from your body is through sneezing. I learned this from the old villagers; a majority of them will never see the walls of a clinic because they provoke sneezing with an herb powder they snuff to provoke a good and powerful sneeze periodically. Until I started studying healing, I thought that was nasty! "Those who do not understand the rhythm and language of the drums call it noise (African proverb)." Let your nose run for a day before you start taking antihistamines if inclined to. Let the dreg come out of you! You will progressively get fewer colds! (Yes, I take tips ☺)

Talking about techniques, get the technique right.
Master it first; don't cheat (yourself) if the technique is tough, as
in starting an exercise program for example. Once mastered, build
on it and now you can go faster. Many people give up on things
later in life because a tiny little point was not mastered at the
right stage. Now they have a high paying job, game, etc. but that
Achilles heel keeps rearing its head. This brings much
unhappiness. Hunker down and learn. Stick with it; the training
gets easier and will soon be over!

Read all the instructions. (Similar as above point.)
Sometimes we are unhappy while we have all the tools and
resources, and do not know it because we want shortcuts and
have not read the manual and **instructions**. Find the instructions
for relationships and whatever makes you unhappy and read
them so your next experience will be different. Your closet
already has what you are dying to (re) buy.

Know Thyself (see *"Cracking the Code; The Path to Creating a
Successful Life. Powerful Tools to Bring about Life Fulfillment."* A
Home Study Coaching Program at www.estherlamnyam.com.)
Invest time in self-knowledge, as you are the genesis and the
coffin to all that will ever happen to you.

Example: Relationship breakups cause a lot of unhappiness,
especially when we do not know ourselves (and repeat with
different people). To clarify this aspect of self-knowledge, let me
offer you this story. Years ago, in the eighties, a great soldier
came to me in tears, depressed, upset because of a broken
relationship. He could not sleep or eat. What I remember from my

conversation with him is this, I said to him, "but you agreed to breakup your relationship with your girlfriend." In solemn, teary eyed, teary voiced, painful body language, he responded with this statement that I have never forgotten, "but I did not know I was going to feel this way!"

He did not know himself. If he did know he would hurt like breakups do, would he not have broken up? I do not know. What I can offer now that I am more vested in helping others find joy, is that he would have prepared himself for the painful outcome, or eased out of the relationship, or worked hard on making it work, or best of all do the work needed before he got into any kind of relationship where there is another entity involved. Nature my biggest teacher, has taught me that human beings are **Beings** being! Get it? We are constantly changing!

A friend years ago always called me and told me the psychic for sure said she will get married in May, or December, or meet the man here or there for sure, etc. Ten years later the story had different permutations but the same outcome – still single. I observed she was not the only one with this failed relationship outcome, even though the psychics were cock sure.

So I meditated on this ...why Pops, why? Short answer is we are spiritual beings in a physical body! Both aspects of us have rules that apply and are constantly in motion, like the clouds in the sky. Many pay attention to an infinitesimally limited nonsensical part of the physical (case in point those who swoon over abs, other body parts, and money, and marry a person for that) without trying to get a little grasp on the interconnectedness of these *beings* (self-included.) Traffic, both earthly and celestial, affects this being; wireless communications (thoughts, mind, etc.) affects this being; the physical biology and earth physics like

126

gravity, affects this being. Culture, tribalism, sexism ("oh I wish you were a boy or girl",) paid or unpaid bride price, ancestral worship all the way to Abram aka Abraham, affects this being. Colonization affects this being, (shut up ego!). Migrations, guilt, greed, color, secret addictions, religious brainwashing, "I can do bad all by myself," affects this being. Men brought up without a father to inoculate them with male energy so they are vaccinated against their own ego and primordial rebellion, affects this being (even Jesus needed an earthly papa! Hello!). Degeneration of anything made of ground/dust, affects this being. Need we discuss any more why the psychics need psychics? "Man" is fluid within and without! (Yes, tip ☺)

We all want our desires to manifest; though results are abysmal in many cases. Change is mother earth's code. However, we must understand the interconnectedness of the universe in multi-dimensions to make better progress.

Whatsoever thou resolvest to do, do it quickly. Defer not till the evening what the morning may accomplish. - Unto Thee I Grant. Procrastination, distractions, sweet television programs have cost many people pain and their future. Make rules and honor them; in college when I became a victim of this, I promised my alarm clock I will honor it and I did...most of the time in tears, literally and a swollen face, as four hours of sleep was a luxury.

The only thing you can keep when you give out is your word, even given to yourself. Be mindful of the words or promises you make. People count on them, especially children! You corrode your credibility when you do not keep your word, (e.g. I'll be right back; I will call you later; I'll show up for your game). Corrosion takes years to be evident, but by then there is no fiber to rebuild on! But do not misunderstand this point and be bullied or manipulated (even with books like the Bible and/or cultural norms.) If you change/renew your mind, **give feedback**. Release others. Happy? You/they will feel/know it when you come from a place of love.

Promises of marriage made to many African girls have them now *miserable,* as the men went abroad or to the cities and never returned. They waited! Now they are older 'broken' maids. Ahh, the years of tortured anticipation and hormonal suppression! Sob, sob, and sob.

Live with joy, live with love, live with gratitude. Choose to and watch the universe unfold beauty to you! Loose complaining ...for good.

128

Be Truthful. Tell the truth. Tell the truth to...YOU!

Many of us are liars (okay let me speak for myself). Be truthful, else all this good stuff I share with you will be hard to come to *grounded* fruition. Once I discovered I was a liar, I can say that was my first real conscious initiation into the beginning of *clarity*. To make this point real quick, I'll explain by way of an experience that changed my life. While it is about me, however, it is a universal story since it helped start me on this journey of *"becoming"*. I pray it helps you deeply, so open your heart to it.

More than twenty years ago, I was involved with an organization...all expatriates in the U.S. The goal was to do community projects in Africa and to have a community to hang out in. A lady joined this organization and befriended us (woman again; hehehe). Eventually, she became quite contrary to many and me, changing rules even when she had not shown up for meetings and somehow 'forcing' the leaders to accept them. If I commented, I got into trouble. I started noticing that when she called me, I lost my joy and even my appetite. I sincerely tried to babysit her emotions and whims; but the more I tried, the more she abused me. I prayed about it without much result, I thought. I was so afraid of meeting her at an upcoming wedding that I had this brilliant idea to ignore her. I did not know at the time, but this idea would be the thread I needed to be initiated into a higher grade of my spiritual life.

I greeted her at the wedding then proceeded to stay away from her, never commenting on her stories to save myself. Guess what! This pissed her off. First lesson, evil is very aware of energy and what it is doing. Evil needs attention. Well, as a true human (forget the 'being'), I said "ah ha, now I finally have something I

129

can do to you to hurt you after all these months that you have been whipping my butt, hehehe."

So yes, I ignored her now with purpose. Enjoy! Well she went into overdrive of her negative actions towards me and I withered under the stress of it like a leaf under sun without water! Sob! Sob!

One Saturday morning, I was on my knees praying, "Oh Pops, save me from this woman, she is causing havoc in my life and I have not done anything to her. I helped her with this, that, etc." I told my Pops how I have been accommodating to her, even taking care of the responsibilities her boyfriend normally did, but couldn't do while travelling that she asked me to do for her like drop her at school and work.

After my prayer, I had breakfast and started vacuuming the floor. This is when it happened! In my mind, I started enjoying how pissed off she was that I ignored her. I was joyous that I had finally found something that could get under her thick evil skin. I smiled to myself, vacuumed and then started talking to My Higher Self (you know how you answer your own troubleshooting...master mind with yourself!) and here is how the conversation went:

"Brilliant idea to ignore her. I am so glad she is pissed. Good; now she can feel some pain."

"But I thought you just told God you did nothing to her." My higher self (I would call it) said,

"Yes, I did nothing to her; she is always the one, irritating me with xyz." I responded. Then I told my conscious self, she was really pissed when I did not engage in her story at the wedding. She was so pissed that she touched my watch and it stopped working. Who knew just ignoring someone could make them so livid, hehehe!"

"Oh so you ignored her, I thought you just told Pops you did nothing to her and for Him to protect you?" My higher self responded. This conversation went on for maybe one minute or five, as I was vacuuming and enjoying being able to hurt an abuser.

Then as my 'higher self' kept asking me questions, at *one moment,* it dawned on me that I had lied to God (of course God like mom and dad knows we ate the cookie though we say we did not). I realized I could lie to both spiritual and physical parents and all others, but there was one person I could not lie to and that person ALWAYS knew the truth! Me. I. I am.

Nobody knew I was ignoring her...but I knew. No one knew she was pissed but I knew. I had no control over her behavior but I had control over mine. Was I going to go to the dark side and dwell with evil to fight evil? My reaction revealed to me, consciously that I was a liar and that in the spiritual realm there is no *small* negativity...like "ignore," though in the physical it might look like it is *no big deal*! I realized how easy it is to lie to God and keep behavior that is contrary to my success and to the light I could bring to others, as darkness has no choice when light comes but to disappear. Learn to love your neighbor...well love yourself first...then neighbor as self. All we do, we only do unto ourselves.

The choice I made at that moment on how to move forward moved the dial for me a few degrees; it opened spiritual doors to me that helped me begin to see the metaphysical side of the Bible and other spiritual authors. It lead me to a path and journey that has led me to where I am today...on that journey, (the joy is in the **JO**URNEY and not in stagnation). I offer this to you today!

Is telling the truth easy, no! But that is the only way to get to the other side for most of us…maybe you too. If you find another way, please share it with the world. This choice is yours.

Woman, wherever you are, thank you for being whatever! To run from you and from your evil, I ran straight into God's almighty arms, protection, and guidance and it facilitated and accelerated my spiritual illumination …one of my life goals! hehehehehehehe! I say this with a clean heart. It (negativity) was converted or transmuted to good or beauty (as 'good' translates as 'beauty' in the village).

Keep a pure heart and integrity (e.g. King Abimelech in the Bible) and you and yours will be exonerated and be happy.

Take heart; you are not going to be understood, especially if you have 'talent' that is out of the box. Do not try too hard to be understood! Keeping moving and refining your skills and one day it will pay dividends. Young people especially need to bear this in mind. That is why *self*-knowledge and *self*-confidence is so important to develop.

Have Mantras you repeat often and honor. For example, as teens we had mantras that I remember and use till today: "You do good, you only do good to yourself. You do bad, you only do bad to yourself." "Do not say welcome to anything that will be hard to say good bye to." "One minute of pleasure, a lifetime of regrets." This kept us out of trouble…because we took those words to heart. Little sayings like these can ensure your happiness.

Fight fair in relationships; because sometimes when you win in certain relationships, you actually lose. If you have to really "beat" them to make a point or teach a lesson, do it with love and in such a way their honor is not destroyed. If you destroy them and you love them, you will feel their pain and you will be unhappy (in your conquest!) Use common sense always, as there are real evil people out there.

*Do not make a vow or promise and not keep it. Do not make a vow or promise you do not intend to keep. As indicated at the beginning, many people are stuck because of (non-intentional sometimes) energy being levied at them in the form of anger, negative wishes, curses, etc. Typical examples are men who sell the marriage or "together forever" pill to *believing* women, then after physical pleasure, they dump these women; sometimes with babies. The hatred, angry energy through thoughts (aka prayers), words, and action towards these men is enough to launch a nuclear bomb. If you believe in the efficacy of prayer, vision boards, meditation and you realize prayer is really at the 101 level a thought or word spoken, then think what these angry thoughts are doing to these men! Wonder why some really smart guys keep going round and round. We already discussed the power of women, let alone an angry one! She may not even know how powerful her angry thoughts are, but her dispensing them works magic!

Use silence. Touch. Touch your partners and kids. Healing hands. The hand of God! Many illnesses might be a result of people and children not being touched, hugged, and being carried in strollers more than being held. Feed yourself and kids with your fingers sometimes. Imitate the great Master…touch someone (with a healing touch, I mean!).

Changing for others. Storm, a man I befriended told me how he was encouraged by his third wife to be circumcised when in his thirties. (Yes, ouch in caps!) At this age, it is full costly surgery. Well, she left him thereafter. His stories about women were so bitter I distanced myself from him. Not knowing who you are, not setting boundaries and letting people accept you for who you are, can cause unhappiness to many…some still to come in your future.

If people do not love you or reciprocate, leave them alone…else you will waste so much energy and life force. While most of us desire to be loved, at times we just have to cut our losses, cry, and move on. Few die from being single, many die from being coupled!

"I can do bad by myself" – not! It's all about energy. **Explanation by Example -**The radio station story - Girl in Atlanta: There was a radio station I listened to online in the nineties. It had a segment where people called in to find closure in a relationship by asking a former partner why they had been dumped. In one particular episode, a young lady asked the DJ (Disc Jockey) to called three different men who had dumped her when she had thought the relationships were going on well. The DJ called one guy after the other and interestingly they all obliged and answered the question.

What was surprising is that they all had a similar reason for breaking up with her. In each case they liked the girl very much and shortly after starting to date her, she moved in with each of them. Each guy told a similar story. Shortly after she moved in, she removed some of their stuff from the dresser drawers to make room for her stuff. She put their underwear or socks in another drawer. Shortly thereafter, they broke up with her.

Three different guys, called by the DJ separately, had a similar story! She did not get why that mattered; the DJ and his team speculated as to why getting space in the drawers for her lingerie and more would break a relationship. I did not know either and this story queried my mind for years! Do you get it? Think about why for a few seconds before reading on...I'll wait. Years later, I discovered why by connecting the dots! Clap for me!

There is always a person in the house through whom energy flows...law of nature. No matter how much bad you or I (females!) can do by ourselves, the energy flow is not part of that club. In my opinion, it is the male figure even if you partnered with a younger man, illiterate man or the village beggar. So if the person in the house through whom energy should flow is confused, feeling disoriented, not getting the flow, or is in the dog house, only the fleas and the dust will deal with the blessings of this energy. If that person is constantly not happy, the 'household' will constantly be going round and round in cycles. The "start button or switch", might look very tiny or insignificant, yet without it, even the airplane or rocket won't fly higher than its height.

135

When she moved his stuff, in an apartment of balanced energy *for him*, she provoked the funnel spin energy of a tornado. She inevitably reversed the energy flow in the house without knowing it or intending to. The guys lost their bearings and became "confused," and the very state that had made them like her enough to date her was removed. Hence they did not know who she was any more and they asked her to leave! You may be asking how could she have known this or stopped it? Don't know, but we can start with giving honor to people, waiting to be invited, humbling ourselves and our beauty and letting those who are supposed to lead, lead. All the education, beauty, "power of the 'femininity'," etc. that you have cannot circumvent the power of nature. The smallest breeze or wind will knock that mighty relationship upside the head.

Imitate the 'village' mom; lead from behind without giving the semblance of. The egg and the flower look so innocent and helpless, yet the sperm swims to the egg anxiously and the bee flies to the flower hastily. The egg and the flower know their power; hence they know how to pull in their desires without much ado. They do not need to fuss, nor take over control, etc. They are not that innocent and helpless! Know your power and how to use it! Imitate nature to be happy!

I look back at the many women I grew up living with (prep for this work maybe), all those who kept moving the furniture around the house are no longer married or some calamity befell one of the partners! Have you worked with people who when they come on board, must bring their 'hommies' with them and move things and people around? Notice any unhappiness around the corporation? I am a goal setter myself, bucket list and vision board advocate; but I discovered there are subtle "intangibles"

136

that can make or break corporations and mighty alliances. "Those who do not understand the language of the drums, call it noise," - African proverb.

The only two questions you should ask before you start investing any form of energy into a potential life partner, especially for women who want a fulfilling marriage are:

Question to a man you want as a life partner (vice versa):

1(a).) Do you believe in a higher power or being other than you/man?

1(b).) What is your relationship with that power or being?

2(a).) From birth through your teens, were you raised with the presence of a male figure?

2(b/c).) Did that male figure have any practical disciplinary power over you? How did you handle that discipline?

I learned years ago from popular dictions and doctrines, to have a list of things I wanted from a potential partner; needless to tell you that list had been fulfilled many times, yet the relationships failed or did not even attain lift off until I discovered the questions above through lots of prayers. Even Jesus needed an earthly male figure/energy in His life! When we thwart spiritual or natural laws, we inevitably fail miserably and blame entities that have nothing to do with our failure. We even blame 'the devil.' She/he might just screw you up for lying about her/him! Hehehe. This point alone should have you doing a Sarakak if you get it! Remember, I am available for further coaching on points

137

discussed or points your spirit guides you to ask. Man is constantly in evolution, thus 'forces' have to devolution him or dissolution him, as he is a born "rebel" so he stays in "balance" (balance here is not a straight line, more like a sine curve). Now, we see more why happiness is a conscious choice.

Develop and listen to your instinct. Learn from the animals. Be your own "whisperer." Have you ever said of a situation, "I knew it from the moment I met him/her?" "Something told me so"? Just like you get mad when a family member fails and you tell them, "I told you so!" Then do not do to your higher self that goes ahead and scans people and situations for you and whispers to you on first contact with those people and situations the Truth about them, the same thing. Develop your instincts and do not let energies like lust, impatience, non-preparation, and cultural mindsets override. "Truth is slow, but it always arrives" a Wimbum proverb.

Too much knowledge, too soon. That knowledge is too vast for me! In today's relationship world, there is a trend to put all your cards on the table on initial contact. Imitate nature…tell people more about you slowly. Give people time to digest the prelims (preliminaries) then add more. Telling someone all your past conquests, or war killings is too much for starters. The person has not yet absorbed elements of you and harmonized them to move further. Remember, too much bright light to the eyes once in darkness can blind! (If we knew all about God we would not awe Him. Look what was done to Jesus – God in human form!) Hunters lose interest in the hunted once caught…it is like art...to an artist. The soul needs to be constantly tantalized to stay expectant, creative, and juicy!

Understand there are seven levels to the intimacy protocol just like the TCPIP (Transmission Control Protocol/Internet Protocol) stack in computers. Do not confuse the physical lust stage or the emotional stage with the higher ethereal/application levels of relationship in any arena. (I explore this more in my "Cracking the Code on Intimacy" seminars.)

This confusion or lack of knowing has led to many failed relationships. (Adam never gave God the chance to give him instructions and rules for the relationship or to even offer Eve to him per the Bible.) So man is constantly crying, begging, writing, and singing songs about woman, going to war, and some even beating her. He has no clue what to do with her...the very blueprint for his success. He makes up stuff like flowers, diamonds, songs, gifts, "yes dear", because he was too excited to wait for instructions. Those who know what she brings to the table honor her. All highly successful men since Abraham have done so in the company of "woman", even Jesus! Hello! Hidden in plain sight!

Marriage as we know it today, in the West, especially, is a contract between the State government and a man and woman; and between them and children. Harmonizing or Spiritual marriage has no need for written contracts! Contracts do get broken (man-made that is.)!

All through the Bible, God always gives step-by-step instructions; however, in the case of *His coming around to Adam with Eve* a major phase in His plan, no documented instructions!

139

Hmmm! Adam rushed to, "Wo," "Waoh" Wo-man. Notice how God shut up His own mouth!? Hehehe.

Get a coach. You have heard me say this many times in this book, as it will accelerate your growth. Years of experience will have a good mechanic knowing what is wrong just by hearing the sound without even opening the hood to fix your car. He will fix your car in less than 30 minutes. You probably wasted time, happiness, frustration, and money trying to do it yourself or going to quack mechanics. Do not take pills that give you headaches and high blood pressure… **Invest in a coach.** This will make your efforts productive, and save you lots of money, time, and frustration. Conversations with friends for feedback is good; reading books is necessary, but sometimes you need a hands-on coach to be able to implement with efficacy the technique the book is teaching.

The tools are all over in congregations, online, in books, and here therein. You have the key within. You say, "but I know and I have these tools and the key; why am I fumbling; what else do I need?" Hummm, someone to show you the keyhole! The right coach for your desire! Seek and you will find…seek you must first…to find; ask and it shall be given …ask first; knock and it shall be opened; knock first. When *it* knows you are seeking with passion, chances are *it* will find you (by making you find *it*).

The happiness song! Sing happy songs. Happy music and stories and televisions will help keep you happy. We sang this song below in middle school a gazillion years ago, but I draw on it periodically to juice up. There are tools within, find and use them.

(Hint: use the Bible and other religious books as self-help tools if nothing else. They have stood the test of time! You do not have to belong to that religion. People of religions different from ours write many great self-help books and music that help us. We are all connected. The Bible is read and respected by many so I use it more to illustrate so we all have a common denominator to learn /extrapolate from :)!

Happiness song:
Happiness Is

Happiness is to know the Savior,
Living a life in His favor,
Having a change in my behavior
Happiness is the Lord.

Happiness is a new creation.
Jesus and me in close relation
Having a part in His salvation
Happiness is the Lord.

Real joy is mine
No matter if teardrops start;
I've found the secret,
It is Jesus in my heart.

Happiness is to be forgiven
Living a life that's worth the livin'
Taking a trip
That leads to heaven
Happiness is the Lord

Happiness is the Lord
Happiness is the Lord

Conclusion - Mind "The Intersection".

As discussed in this text, there are lots of books, formulas, music, tweets, abs, stilettos, tools, workshops, diamonds, shoes, villas, money, etc. to make us happy. However, though some of us do the obvious like goal setting, vision boards, bucket lists, win money, marry princes and princesses, you name it, yet sometimes we still are unhappy, as these things do not hit the spot.

When we violate the intersection of the spirit and the physical, those tools eventually die a natural death. We thus need a little spice to make it all come alive. The tools I share with you in here will move the needle for you in the direction of happiness if you use them. You may in them find just one "spice" that you use over and over to juice up!

When our energy is low because we are not happy, we cannot be very productive. We suffer, family suffers, the cooperation, and the country suffers. We need each other and we need your talent just as you need mine. The all is in the one and the one is in the all.

As spiritual beings using a physical apparatus to live life, we need to always be conscious of the intersections and the interconnectedness of our words, deeds, thoughts, daily, hourly, and minutely. Choose to be happy and use these tools developed from putting an ear to the ground and listening, getting into tiny gabs of issues to figure out why there are issues, and discovering the threads needed to fix them.

I trust these tips serve you. As indicated at the beginning, feedback from the blog post I wrote necessitated me adding more tools to the list in the blog. So please I await your feedback. My desire is to serve you at your point of need; email me your challenges and let's get some more spice (tools) for your journey.

I trust these key points on engineering happiness have served you and yours. What I know, I share with you. If you need follow-up coaching or teaching on these points for you or your organization contact me at info@ImitateNature.com or through my website www.estherlamnyam.com. You are also invited to sponsor or spread the word about some of my humanitarian initiatives - in 2001 I started The Njuh Scholarship Fund sponsoring elementary schools kids in the village (http://estherlamnyam.com/out-reach). In 2012 I started a new mentoring and coaching effort to teach African middle school students self-growth so they can become self-reliant, and turn around and help their village, country, and the world. Here are some videos links of me speaking to them: http://youtu.be/4Bp-ngEkkAQ, http://youtu.be/j9eVUVFp_TY. Also, read blogs on my website for more tips for your wellness and life success strategies.

The key is that it is a partnership; it is teamwork. We are co-creators with the spiritual world; with God. "Ask, and it shall be given to you; seek, and ye shall find; knock, and it shall be opened unto you." One additional commandment I give you, "give and it shall be given to you." Imitate nature. Do the work! We have a part to play no matter how much we pray or meditate or use vision boards.

Live with Joy, Live with Love, Live with Gratitude.

Appendix

Travaux Practique = Practical application, homework, or lab work.

Why Irretrievably? In some of the cases used as examples, I say the relationship broke up "irretrievably." You might ask why irretrievably? This is because at any given moment, "life goes on." When there are issues and people delay really working on them or they do so intermittently, other "issues, entities, and rhythms," flow in and inevitably change the dynamics. When the persons involved eventually get together to work on the issue, they have these layers of things that are not obvious but impact the relationship. There is never "empty" space.

As an example, say best friends Emily and Prisca are fighting over Emily not inviting Prisca to Emily's baby shower. Emily's friends made the mistake. Emily tries to contact Prisca, but Prisca stalls, she has the upper hand and is playing it!

By the time Prisca enjoys her anger and comes around to talking with Emily, Emily has had the following and more happen to her:

- Her husband lost his job. He feels down and she has to comfort him.
- First child is teething, has diarrhea, and she is taking off work too often.
- Boss getting worried as she can't finish present deadlines before maternity leave and now first child's illness is making her take off more days.

144

- She is sleeping less and her doctor wants her more often at his office for checkups, as she is due soon to have the second child.
- The dog needs to see the vet, and the husband can't do it as he is out job interviewing. She has to do it on limited time.
- Groceries, laundry, birthday invitations, baby sitter issues.
- Her hormones are going crazy, yet her husband for a while now has refused to make love to her claiming the baby might be watching from within or he might hurt the baby. He does not believe the doctors. She starts getting migraines and she is not even allowed medication.
- In-laws and parents call often for travel arrangements and follow-ups about their impending visit when she has baby.
- Mood swings, constipation, some astrological stuff is going on.
- It's a full moon. It's too cold. It's too hot. Furloughs are being discussed on the job.
- Etc. etc.

By this time, Prisca is not on Emily's mind, as issues with Prisca are now layers beneath what she is dealing with.

Prisca is approaching Emily at the same level as months ago but Emily is miles away trying to manage kids, her husband, the upcoming birth, work issues, and more. In Emily's mind now,

145

Prisca can go eat dung. Earlier she had been ready to kiss Prisca's derrière to resolve this issue.

Basically, life, nature, and seasons flow in and people deal with life; and when others show back up on the scene, they are meeting someone who has evolved at many levels. Energy has changed, minds renewed, planetary cycles influences, growth has happened, life and death happens. Thus the relationship is irretrievably changed. The Good book says do not go to bed with issues not resolved. The night or darkness is a place of growth in the "negative" direction. Let things go. Strive to be happy!

Esther Lamnyam's Biography

Esther is a gifted visionary Wellness, and Life Success Strategist, who works with women (and men) interested in building long lasting relationships with self and others by claiming/reclaiming their spiritual, physical, emotional life, health, and wellness using different modalities, techniques, and African healing traditions and wisdom.

Esther helps clients see the interconnected of their life and uses different tools to assist them create their desired success. She shows them how to create fulfilling relations by using the laws of nature, which cannot be looped-holed, bribed, or manipulated in any physical court of law and helps them find their personal success code. Many have said, "She fixes at the root."

Esther Lamnyam donates a portion of the proceeds from the sale of her works and books to *The Njuh Scholarship Fund* founded in 2001, to send disadvantaged village kids to school. She also travels to Africa periodically to mentor and coach youths on self-growth so they can develop tools for their own success. She welcomes anyone willing to sponsor these projects. She can be contacted by sending an email to info@ImitateNature.com and through her website: www.estherlamnyam.com.

Esther is a consultant, coach, speaker, writer, iridologist, healer, and Information Technology Systems Architect. Esther is

147

the founder of Imitate Nature Consulting, and Coaching International, and The Entrée and Dance Club. She is the author of the books: "Love Under the Kola Nut Tree. What City Moms Didn't Tell You About Creating Fulfilling Relationships," "My Husband Is A Cuckoo: And Other Poems of my Youth," available on amazon.com: http://tinyurl.com/n6juwx6.

Some of Esther's credentials: she is certified as: an Iridologist, Herbal Counselor, Usui Reiki L1 healer, Network Administrator and IBM Lotus Domino Engineer, Fowler Wainwright International Institute of Professional Coaching Certified Professional Coach, and A Commissioned Stephen Minister. Esther has a M.S. degree in Management of Information Systems from the University of Akron, Akron Ohio, and a B.Sc. in Computer Science from Spelman College, Atlanta, Georgia. She is also a spiritual teacher and student, with nature being one of her teachers. Esther was born in Cameroon and has lived in the United States for the greater part of her life.

To hire Esther Lamnyam for speaking engagements or coaching and consulting, contact her through her website **www.estherlamnyam.com** or by sending an email to info@ImitateNature.com.

Made in the USA
Middletown, DE
05 June 2015